Dont Give Up
On Love
The ultimate guide to
bringing happiness
into your marriage.

Don't Give Up On Love

On Love
The ultimate guide to bringing happiness into your marriage.

JOSEPH L. FOLLETTE JR.

ARPress
ILLUMINATING IDEAS,
EMPOWERING VOICES

ARPress
45 Dan Road Suite 5
Canton MA 02021

Hotline: 1(888) 821-0229
Fax: 1(508) 545-7580

Ordering Information:
Quantity sales. Special discounts are available on quantity purchases by corporations, associations, and others. For details, contact the publisher at the address above.

Printed in the United States of America.

ISBN-13:   Softcover   979-8-89356-538-6
           eBook   979-8-89356-539-3

Library of Congress Control Number: 2024902457

TABLE OF CONTENTS

ACKNOWLEDGEMENTS

I want to, first of all, give glory and honor to God for inspiring me to write this book. I also want to thank Him for using me to be a blessing to so many people all these years.

I want to thank all of my clients who took the risk of talking to a stranger about their problems. I am grateful for all the expressions of appreciation through the years. This book is dedicated to all of my clients whose stories have inspired me.

Finally, I'm grateful to my wife, Claudia, who has taught me so much about love and marriage.

FOREWORD

The universe isn't held together by atoms. The essential binding element is love. When God sought to correct the biggest problem in the universe (man's separation from God) he used love. It's unstoppable.

Love is glue. Love is camouflage. Love is GPS. Love is a magnet.

God wants us to experience the power of love. But love is a skill. It is a commitment. It's not merely the culmination of "chemistry".

Marriage was given to us so we could learn, experience, and share love.

I've known Joe for most of my life. He's always cared deeply about love and helping people experience it at ever deeper levels. It's his calling.

As such he has written a book that is rooted in helping you love, really love the person God has given you.

What I love most about what you're going to experience as you work through these pages is he calls you to "be". This is about developing the mindset to make love sizzle.

It's one thing to learn some techniques or tricks. But that's not love. That's just trying to find the right buttons to push to get what YOU want.

The last thing two people need to build an eternity together is mutual manipulation.

No, Joe calls us to collaborate.

And that collaboration starts with a commitment to "be" the love we need and to inspire our partner to grow into the glorious person God has called them to become. The process of becoming requires tools, coaching, and effort. It's all here.

There are some estimates that 2 billion people watched the royal wedding of William and Kate. Do you remember the sermon? I don't think anyone really does. But Archbishop Rowan Williams spoke with power and clarity.

He said, "Marriage should transform, as husband and wife make one another their work of art. It is possible to transform as long as we do not harbor ambitions to reform our partner. There must be no coercion If the Spirit is to flow; each must give the other space and freedom."

Joe gives us the tools to "be" the kind of partners that succeed and sizzle in our marriages.

I've found his words inspiring, important, challenging, and essential.

Take the time to read, reflect and try.

These tools will bind you, cover you, give you direction and draw you to each other and the heart of God.

This isn't just a book, it's a playbook for new beginnings.

Hallerin Hilton Hill

(Hallerin is author of The Seven Pillars of Wisdom, a talk show host on Newstalk 98.7 WOKI and Anything is Possible on WBIR-TV in Knoxville, Tennessee, a songwriter, singer, motivational speaker, and trainer.)

PREFACE

Having crossed many milestones at this point in my life, it is so exciting to see young people anticipating completing first grade, high school, college, graduate school, getting married, having their first child, a new job, etc. But I've come to realize they are not always aware of the challenges that accompany each milestone in marriage. Finding someone to love is a wonderful milestone. Yet as so many have found, the challenges that come with marriage can be overwhelming. In this book, I share some valuable lessons that will help and guide you through the many obstacles married couples face on their life journey together. I will teach you how to *return to love* when the going gets tough. I want to encourage you to not give up on love. You can have the marriage of your dreams if you refocus on your mindset and happiness, rather than trying to figure out and fix the mindset and behaviors of your spouse. I want you to learn how to bring happiness into your marriage.

I write from serving as a counselor in many different roles. I have counseled as a church pastor, college professor, men's dormitory dean, marriage and family therapist in private practice, college student counselor, substance abuse counselor, and crisis counselor. In my private practice, I've counseled men and women, boys and girls across the lifespan, hundreds of couples, gay and straight, single and married, dealing with myriads of issues and challenges. I've worked with families in poverty and the top one percent of income earners. I've run anger management groups, shyness groups, ADHD groups for kids, drug cessation groups, divorce care groups, sex addiction groups, abuse recovery groups, and marriage groups. I've been on many stages teaching and preaching marriage and family education. I counsel from the perspective of being a third-generation Seventh-day Adventist pastor, twice married with five kids with a blended family.

As a marriage & family therapist, I work from a systems perspective, considering the intrapsychic and interpersonal context of individual and relationship problems. I offer additional services to address the individual issues that often complicate interpersonal issues. It has been a blessing to me to have been able to advise, motivate, and bring healing to thousands of people over the years. Writing books, blogs, and social media posts have been an additional avenue to educate and encourage the masses.

While I counsel individuals, marital relationships have been my primary focus over the years. It breaks my heart to see love wasted and family's crumble. Whatever I can do to keep another family together, I'm in. I've been keeping families strong by helping couples address and resolve the issues that threaten their marriage and teaching them how to communicate effectively. I hope this book will help you see what you are doing wrong in your marriage and show you how to turn things around. While what is written in this book is not intended to replace therapy, it certainly can go a long way to help you address the issues that threaten your peace, joy, and happiness together. You will vicariously enter the therapy room as I share the experience of my fictitious couple, Ryan and Tiffany.

The difficulties in marriage stem from the baggage we bring into the marriage. All of us have been wounded and shaped by various negative experiences. An absent father or an emotionally distant mother can have a devastating impact on our beliefs and perceptions of others and ourselves. Our parents' trauma trickles down to us. We naturally inherit many of their tendencies and hang-ups. This baggage affects how we interpret and respond to things our partner says and does. The greatest challenge couples experience is trying to understand and interpret each other positively. Couples who have the most problems were often raised so fundamentally different that they are unable to comprehend each other's perspective and way of thinking. That is why an interpreter is needed to decipher the deeper meanings, unpack the baggage, and help couples create a new language so they can understand each other and live together in peace. I've been blessed to be that interpreter for thousands of couples over the years.

To have a whole marriage, you must have two whole people. I aim to help each individual take responsibility for their contribution to the breakdown of the relationship, recognize their flaws, and work on themselves rather than focus on the flaws in their mate. At the end of the day, you can only change yourself. So hopefully, as you read this book, you will read it not just within the context of improving your marital relationship, but your own personal development and growth.

Maybe as you read this book, you recognize how your baggage is negatively affecting your marital relationship(s). I hope this book can help you on your healing journey. If you realize you need more help, check out https://SizzlingHotMarriage.com to see if there is something I'm offering that seems to be what you are needing right now. Let's begin unpacking your baggage and getting the healing you need so you can be your best self and the marital partner that contributes to a strong and healthy relationship.

In this book, I share the story of Ryan and Tiffany, a fictitious couple who, even with some extreme challenges, were able to take their marriage from cold to *Sizzling Hot*. They decided they were not willing to give up on their love. They learned how to refocus on themselves and transformed their marriage. They chose to fix their marriage rather than throw it out.

CHAPTER ONE
The Introduction

I'm old enough to remember hearing "ice man" being yelled in the early hours of the morning. My dad would rush out of the campground cabin we were residing to buy some ice for the icebox. If we wanted to keep our food from spoiling, we needed ice in the icebox. While electric refrigerators were readily available, our campground decided to hold on to the old iceboxes a little while longer.

Has your marriage lost its warmth and gotten a little chilly? Are you barely talking to each other? Has sex become a distant memory? Maybe you are looking around at other couples who appear to be having a great time and wondering why your marriage has to be so hard. Has your marriage become that old icebox that you are seriously considering throwing out? May I suggest that your old icebox may still have some life left in it?

Ryan and Tiffany were an attractive young couple in their early thirties when they came to see me. They looked like they were perfectly matched for each other. I have a theory that people are attracted to those who share similar physical attributes. These two complemented each other so well. They met while attending a small Christian college in town, not far from where my office was located. It was many years after college, after they had established their careers that they reconnected and fell in love. Married just two years when I met them, they still loved each other deeply. But they found themselves in a struggle they weren't sure how to navigate.

They didn't have big fights with loud yelling and name-calling. They would just go back and forth obviously agitated with each other. It seemed like everything became a big debate. They struggled to get along and truly enjoy each other's company. Over time their marriage lost the meaning they once enjoyed, and they found themselves just going through the motions. Drowning in discord, dissatisfaction, and disappointment, they finally got professional help.

Here's a couple that started *Sizzling Hot.* They were excited to be together. They were friends. They spoke to each other with warmth and love. They worked through conflict easily as they listened to each other and discussed their different ideas like mature in-love adults. They peered into each other's eyes as they spoke to one another. They responded warmly and with understanding. They cherished each other. They touched each other in an affectionate way frequently throughout the day. They were deeply attracted to each other and had sex several times each week. But they soon realized falling in love and getting married was the easy part. Figuring out how to live together peacefully and stay in-love was the hard part.

The conflict arose as they discovered how very different, they were. As the days and weeks from the wedding passed, their conflict threw cold water on their *Sizzling Hot* flame.

Before they got married, they couldn't get enough of one another. During the honeymoon phase, they did everything together. But as they faced the issues and each other's hang-ups, they began to experience frustration and disappointment as their hopes for their union seemed to be unrealizable. Their positive opinion of who they had selected as a life mate began to wane. They began to see things in one another's personality and character that was simply annoying.

Ryan said that Tiffany was controlling. He had spent many years living on his own going through college and medical school. He was used to doing things his way. He went to bed and got up when he felt like it. He took care of business. He didn't need anyone coaching him. And when he was ready to relax and unwind from a hard day's work, he didn't need anybody telling him what to do or how to do it. As an avid sports fan, his way of relaxing was sitting in his recliner, captivated by the late-night games and sports commentary. Because he loved almost every sport, this was a year-round obsession. Every chance he got; he was reading about sports. He had his regular nighttime routine that he didn't expect to be disturbed once he got married. Tiffany nagged him about coming to bed at a decent hour. She felt like he was not getting enough sleep. She also felt like he was avoiding her. She was beginning to feel alone. She felt like she had to find things to do to occupy herself while he occupied himself with sports. But little did she know that Ryan's "sports" time was not just for sports. Ryan was watching it without her. It began to dawn on her that Ryan had a problem with porn. While he was in his own world enjoying the game, he would entertain himself by looking at provocative pictures of naked women performing sexually with men. He was using sports time as his cover for his obsession with pornography on his phone or laptop.

Pornography had been Ryan's entertainment beginning at 12 years of age when he discovered an X-rated videotape of his dads. Since he was a latchkey kid, he would occasionally watch the video when he came home from school. His brother soon joined him in this newfound entertainment. Together they procured their own stash of pornographic material. Ryan had been consuming porn for over 15 years before meeting and marrying Tiffany. In fact, Ryan was so fascinated with porn that he introduced it to Tiffany as a prop to heat up their sex life. Even though Tiffany was raised as a much more than Ryan, she didn't think their sex porn was a problem. They were married now, and they could do whatever worked for them, she believed. Tiffany didn't hold it against him because she believed all guys look at porn and really didn't see any harm in it. She didn't need it but, if this was what he wanted to do, she was cool with it. She didn't realize how pervasive his dependency was and how negatively it would impact their relationship.

Tiffany began to experience Ryan as distant and not really interested in her. She began to feel like what she felt, and thought was not important to him. She felt like he was always brushing her off. She became more suspicious, wondering if he was spending time with someone else. She started paying more attention to his devices to see if she could catch a glimpse of an inappropriate text message, email, or phone call. One night she woke out of her sleep. After checking her phone, she glanced over at Ryan and saw that he was watching porn. Ryan was so engrossed he didn't realize Tiffany had awakened. She was disgusted as she realized Ryan had a dependency on porn. He had led her to believe it wasn't a problem. That it was something, he occasionally did with her when they were having sex. She asked him what he was doing.

Seeing that he was busted, Ryan didn't have any good explanation. So, he proceeded to defend himself using sarcasm, "What does it look like I'm doing?" Tiffany was hurt and concluded that this is what he was doing every night and that this is the reason he was so distracted. Ultimately, Ryan realized his source of entertainment was causing problems in his marriage, so he told her he would quit. However, like any dependency, It wasn't so easy to stop.

Tiffany unconsciously began a campaign to help Ryan to move away from his dependency. She urged him to focus more on her and their relationship. She became very forceful in her efforts to motivate him to make changes. She would remind him when it was time to go to bed and tell him that coming to bed would help him avoid the temptation to look at porn. She would dress up in fancy lingerie working really hard to get his attention.

Ryan wasn't fully on board with her efforts. He experienced her as trying to control him, making him feel like less of a man and like she was mothering him. His aim was to get her to lay off. Her aim was to get him to be a man of integrity so she could feel more confident in his love. Little did they know the war had begun. Every little thing became a big argument. The more she nagged the more he resisted. They began to see each other as adversaries rather than the friends they used to be.

As they both internalized this perception of one another, they sank deeper, into the corners of the house. They were just going through the motions. They said good morning, gave each other a peck as they rushed out the door to work, and repeated the same when they came home. Tiffany cooked and cleaned the house while Ryan took care of the cars and the lawn. They continued to sit together in church and went out to eat. They hung out laughing with their friends as usual. No one knew their marriage was in trouble. Neither did they. They were going on as usual but were not connecting on an intimate level anymore. They were both doing their own thing under the same roof.

After a while their sex life began to show it. Their sexual frequency declined, and Ryan seemed to be having some performance issues. Tiffany worried that Ryan wasn't finding her as attractive as he once did. She didn't worry him so much about having sex as a priority anymore. She started questioning him about everything. She had to have her way with everything. The more insecure she felt in the marriage the more controlling she became. It was after one spat while they were out with friends that Ryan insisted, they must get into therapy. Tiffany was reluctant because she came from a very private family who would never endorse sharing her problems with an outsider. In addition, Tiffany knew she had a lot of issues she wasn't sure she was ready to deal with. Cautiously she consented to go.

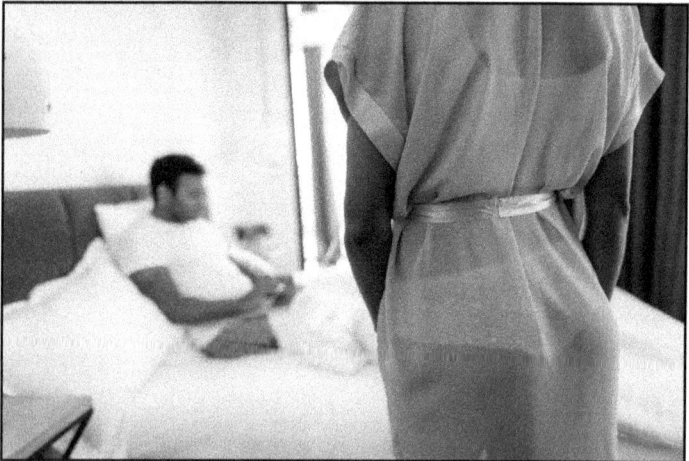

CHAPTER TWO
Therapy

Ryan and Tiffany decided they no longer wanted to be in a cold and loveless marriage. They didn't sign up for this. They wanted things back like they were when they decided to get married. They tried talking about it, they argued and fought, they went silent, they wrote notes to each other, they tried going on vacation, they tried marriage retreats, and they talked to their pastor. They had tried everything – except counseling. If you really want something, when you run out of solutions, you'll finally ask for help. So, they made their first appointment and showed up to begin therapy. After doing their research, they agreed to see me.

While both had grown up with significant dysfunction in their families, Tiffany had experienced serious childhood traumas that she had simply buried and not addressed. These experiences created a great amount of insecurity within her which caused her to react to things in a very controlling way. When a person feels insecure, to reduce the stress of the unknown and avoid potential harm, they tend to organize their environment in a predictable manner. This explains why she became so controlling.

Insecurity is the fear of being hurt or losing something you need. Ryan had never really admitted he had a problem with pornography and masturbation. It was just something he did. He didn't realize this sexual entertainment was familiar and brought comfort for his sense of inadequacy – his not feeling good enough. He didn't realize it made him feel secure. As a latchkey kid, he had to grow up fast. His parents worked a lot and left them home alone. As the oldest, he had to take care of his younger brother. He didn't realize not having an adult around played a role in his insecurities. Porn became a way to pass the time and enjoy sexual stimulation. He didn't realize it at the time, but he was falling into a trap that would get in the way of healthy relationship development with his future wife.

While both attempted to address these unresolved issues in therapy, neither was motivated to take personal responsibility for the problem. Instead, they preferred to focus on seeing the other as the problem. Ryan began to feel like I was taking Tiffany's side in therapy as I was helping him look at himself from Tiffany's perspective. He got angry a couple of times and raised his voice in an attempt to redirect the discussion back to the real problem, Tiffany. This made therapy very uncomfortable for all of us. Not really ready to address his issues, Ryan began making excuses about not having time for therapy. After a few sessions, they stopped coming.

It was maybe a year later when I was surprised to see them back on my schedule. I was shocked yet not surprised when Ryan revealed that he had had an affair. Ryan held his head down in shame. This is something he didn't see coming and had no intention of doing. He was a committed Christian and never expected to be in this situation. He shared that the opportunity just presented itself with a woman at work, and he violated his values and took advantage of the opportunity.

Ryan didn't realize that his pornography dependency would progress and that he would eventually carry out these fantasies in real life.

Tiffany was devastated. She couldn't believe Ryan would do such a thing. Her trust in him had completely evaporated. She still loved him but really didn't know what to do now. Should she continue the possibility of being played like a fool and fight for her man? Or should she cut her losses and end the marriage? She decided she loved Ryan and didn't want to lose all she had invested in this relationship. She saw Ryan's sorrow and shame for what he had done and believed he was redeemable. She remembered that God had forgiven her for her sins and didn't want unforgiveness standing in the way of her blessings. Ryan recognized his sin and the pain he had caused Tiffany. He asked God and Tiffany for forgiveness and promised to respect their covenant from this day forward. They both decided their marriage was worth fighting for, so they came back to therapy, hoping to salvage it. This time they were both very motivated to address their own issues as they were beginning to see the part, they each played in the breakdown of their marriage.

Tiffany and Ryan's story is the same story of hundreds of couples' I have seen. They start out *Sizzling Hot*, but when faced with the realities of one another's idiosyncrasies and faults and their own baggage, this flame can incrementally or suddenly be snuffed out. Compatibility and commitment are not enough to navigate the pitfalls of personality disorders, anxiety, depression, anger, addictions, attention-deficit hyperactivity disorder, post-traumatic stress disorder, and myriads of other mental illnesses all of us struggle with to varying degrees from time to time in our lives. However, many couples make it through their dark valleys. They have climbed the rugged mountains of married life to reach the peak of intimacy.

As a marriage therapist, I worked to help Ryan and Tiffany learn what it takes to enjoy a happy marriage. They came to me with ideas and beliefs that produced discord and not peace. They needed a total mindset shift about what it takes to enjoy a mutually satisfying marital relationship. What they learned growing up wasn't producing the outcome they desired. They needed to change their mindset to navigate the rough terrain of marriage in the twenty-first century.

The mindset shift you need often requires identifying the unresolved emotional issues from childhood that often present as irrational thoughts and disruptive behaviors in your relationships. Do you have to have the last word? Do you get angry quickly? Those intense conflicts may have begun from your failure to listen effectively and jumping to conclusions. Often these unproductive behaviors are triggered by childhood fears and conditioning. In therapy, Ryan and Tiffany were able to pull back the layers that covered years of hurt and disappointment. When you process past wounds, you are better able to be less sensitive or triggered when things or people don't do as expected.

Seeking marriage therapy to get to the bottom of issues is essential to get on the other side of your conflict. Not only will it help you improve your relationship dynamics, but it will also help you focus away from each other onto yourself. This is where relationship transformation happens. It begins with ME. You must identify those things within yourself that are causing problems in the way you see and interact with your spouse. Seeing them, is the only way to have any control of your outcomes. As long as you stay focused on your spouse, you will avoid focusing on yourself. As long as you keep saying your spouse is the problem, the longer you will put off making the difference only you can make in your marriage. You must work on yourself within the context of working on the marriage. This is why you must attend marriage counseling together. You'll have some couple sessions and some individual sessions. The couple sessions will reveal your limiting beliefs. The individual sessions will help you focus on changing those limiting beliefs. I've found this approach works best to help couples hold on to love. The challenge of marriage is integrating ME into WE.

CHAPTER THREE
What is a Sizzling Hot Marriage?

What image comes to your mind when you read the term *"Sizzling Hot Marriage?"* Most say they imagine a marriage with frequent fiery sex. It simply is a term that represents a marriage that is working for both of you. Both of your needs are consistently being met. It is being happily married to your best friend who you can share your life. This is what a passionate marriage is made of. No one taught Ryan and Tiffany how to enjoy a happy marriage. Their parents didn't provide the best examples for them. As a social institution, marriage requires social skills. Couples with the highest levels of emotional intelligence tend to enjoy a more fulfilling and satisfying relationship. We develop our relationship skills from our families of origin. Our outlook on life and how we interpret events in our lives draw heavily from our upbringing and those who come before us. Our ability to navigate problems successfully is a matter of how one was equipped to handle problems. If your parents fell apart when problems arose, you are likely to do the same. Happy people make happy homes. You must learn how to make happiness happen if you want a happy marriage.

Marriages can become strained when couples start thinking negatively about each other or their marriage. It's easy to get caught in a spiral of negative thoughts such as: "I'm not good enough for my partner," "My marriage is doomed," "Nothing I do makes any difference," and so on. Couples can find themselves in conversations full of accusations and blame, only recalling disappointments, hurts, and frustrations. Such conversations make it harder to feel connected, safe, and understood in marriage.

In order to keep a marriage strong, couples need to shift their mindset from a limiting one to an empowering one.

Instead of focusing on the problems, couples should focus on solutions. It is very easy to get stuck in a hurt victim mentality that turns you into an abrasive bitter soul always looking for faults in your spouse and others. Couples should quickly stop complaining and look for ways to communicate effectively, appreciate each other, and resolve conflicts. They should establish ground rules, so discussions stop getting out of control. They should prioritize their marriage and make time for date nights and meaningful conversations. To make these changes requires you to change your focus away from how your partner contributes to your unhappiness to the true source of your unhappiness – the way you think.

The benefits of a strong marriage are immense. A marriage with positive communication, connection, and understanding can provide security, understanding, love, joy, companionship, and friendship—all of which are sure to help you live a long healthy life. Marriage is worth investing in and protecting. The marriage mindset of blaming each other will only lead to further damage, but shifting to a mindset of appreciation, understanding, and cooperation can bring true strength to the marriage. Invest in your marriage—you will reap the rewards in many different ways!

A happy marriage requires effort from both partners to maintain a positive relationship. This includes working on communication, resolving conflicts, and spending time together. Couples happy in marriage also have a shared sense of purpose and enjoy mutual support. Unfortunately, marriage problems can arise when couples don't prioritize their relationship and fail to address issues before they become too big. To keep a marriage strong, both parties need to be willing to make changes and learn new skills.

Couples should start by understanding each other's points of view and working towards common goals. It is important to learn how to communicate effectively, practice appreciation and gratitude for each other, and make time for meaningful conversations. But learning how to communicate effectively, practice appreciation and gratitude, are things an individual must learn to do regardless of their external circumstances. You must learn how to communicate effectively, practice appreciation and gratitude whether your spouse does it or not. Have you ever heard the colloquium, the pot calling the kettle black? Too often we call out the sins of our spouse while ignoring the fact that we are guilty of the same things. That is why Jesus told us to be careful when judging others. That same judgment may come back on you. (See Matthew 7:1-2)

Marriage is worth investing in and protecting. The marriage mindset of blaming each other will only lead to further damage, but shifting to a mindset of appreciation, understanding, and cooperation can bring true strength to the marriage.

Invest in your marriage—you will reap the rewards in many different ways! Marriage is an important commitment that requires effort and understanding from both partners. Couples should prioritize marriage by making time for each other, communicating effectively, and resolving conflicts. With a shared mindset of appreciation, understanding, and cooperation, marriage can provide many benefits, such as security, love, joy, friendship, and companionship. Invest in your marriage and take steps to strengthen it daily—you will reap the rewards for years to come!

I have gleaned much from my research and years of experience working with couples. I've discovered how couples in strong happy marriages think, that helps them stay strong and happy. I've also found how unhappy couples think, that keeps them unhappy. If you want a strong and happy marriage, you must think happy and positive thoughts about your marriage, your spouse, and yourself. Your attitude will determine your altitude.

As a marriage and family therapist, I work to help couples work through their negative experiences and negative beliefs to discover positive thoughts and positive solutions to getting their needs met by each other. Couples in strong, happy marriages establish Community, and Consistency. These are the five pillars upon which a strong marriage stands. These pillars form a foundation for a strong marriage. There are ten mindset shifts you need to make to form these five pillars: Be Hopeful, Be Committed, Be Flexible, Be Available, Be Calm, Be Sexy, Be Talkative, Be Healthy, Be Mindful, and Be God-Centered. If you want to keep the passion alive in your marriage, you must maintain a positive mindset and behavior toward your spouse. These five pillars and ten mindsets will help you stay connected through the busy and dry seasons of life. You can use these principles to get your marriage on the right track and climb to the next level. You will learn in the next few pages how to enjoy a *Sizzling Hot Marriage* by building this five-pillar foundation for your marriage and making these *Sizzle Mindset* shifts. You can have the kind of marriage you signed up to have. You can have a *Sizzling Hot Marriage.* A marriage with connection and understanding can provide security, love, joy, companionship, and friendship— all of which have been scientifically proven to improve physical and mental health.

CHAPTER FOUR
CREDIBILITY

BE HOPEFUL & BE COMMITTED

The first foundational pillar of a *Sizzling Hot Marriage* is Credibility. Credibility comes when others believe in you. They believe that you will do what you say you will do. They know that your yes is yes, and your no is no. This pillar represents your character as a person. If you lack credibility, it will be difficult for your spouse to believe in you. Because marriage is built on trust, without credibility, your marriage will fall apart. Credibility is built with honesty and openness. Credibility is destroyed by deceit, criticism, and neglect. Credibility is a complex concept that includes your trust in each other and yourself to keep your agreements. Trust encompasses many categories, including monogamy, companionship, support, time together, family and friends, spirituality, decision-making, affection, sex, finances, fun, parenting, etc. The agreements couples make include understanding and being respectful of each other, working together to resolve conflicts, making time for each other, supporting each other's goals, working together to keep the house clean, being open about finances and dealing with others, and committing to communicating effectively. Couples trust each other to various degrees on each of these agreements.

It is important to remember that marriage is a commitment that requires effort from both partners over the long haul. When you started dating, you were trying to figure out if this person would be a keeper. You were constantly evaluating your feelings about them and their feelings about you. Over a short or long period of time, you developed agreements with one another and determined how trustworthy each other would be to endure a lifetime commitment to meeting your needs and expectations. The agreements you form, form the marital bond. This bond is not easily broken once formed. It is amazing how couples who have experienced serious challenges like serial infidelity, domestic violence, and substance abuse survive with their marital bond in tack. Many get married not taking into consideration the "for better for worse" clause will be tested in their marriages. Trust can be broken. But it can be rebuilt.

Couples divorce for many reasons. But usually, it involves the breakdown of the marital bond over time or instantly with an egregious betrayal. The marital bond is unique to each couple but involves a connection that is built upon a couple's love story and the agreements they have established to love, support, trust, understand, agree, and form their identity as a couple. This bond includes expectations of what loving each other looks like. When couples keep their agreements, they experience great satisfaction in their relationship. When these agreements are mismanaged, commitment to fulfill the agreements flitters away. When these agreements are no longer held sacred, the marital bond vanishes. Your credibility in your marriage is your confidence that you will keep those agreements and meet each other's needs. Credibility is the ground-level pillar of a strong marriage.

Ryan and Tiffany loved each other deeply but their constant conflict ate away at their credibility with each other. They were unable to communicate in a way to gain understanding and agreement. Over time they simply stopped communicating positivity with each other. They communicated their negative beliefs and feelings about each other. It's difficult to feel troubled in your spirit without communicating, directly or indirectly, those negative emotions to each other. This negativity went totally against Ryan and Tiffany's agreement to love and adore each other. As a result, the fragile thread of their marital bond began to unravel.

When conflict drags on, the temptation to share your woes with others outside your sacred circle is often unbearable. It is very common for couples to form allegiances and confide in others outside that circle, in order to garner support and maybe to get those missing needs met. This is the point when so many couples fall prey to outside influences which creates even more problems for their struggling marriage.

Tiffany chose to talk to her mom about her troubles. Her mother was so understanding and encouraging. If felt good for her to get things off her chest. But she didn't realize the damage she was doing to her marriage by making someone outside her marriage her confidant. Ryan started talking to a woman at work. Little did he know what damage that was causing his marriage. Allowing others into your sacred circle is a betrayal of your marital bond and will further damage the marital bond and make it even more difficult to reconcile and reconnect. It is critically important for you to confide in a professional to help you work through your conflict. I don't recommend going to two different therapists. It is best to seek out a therapist who specializes in marital relationships, can see you individually, and can see you as a couple. It is possible two different therapists are taking you in two different directions. Even if you are planning to go your separate ways, the same therapist can facilitate a more amicable separation. Family and friends are not equipped to help youaddress the complexities of marital conflict. I found that even as a church pastor, I wasn't equipped to help couples navigate the complexities of their conflict. That is why I went back to school to learn how.

A dual relationship is a concept I learned in school that highlights the importance of keeping things simple and not counseling people you have another type of relationship with. Similar to why surgeons don't operate on their family members, it isn't wise for a counselor to counsel family members, neighbors, or classmates. Dual relationships can lead to conflict of interests and power imbalances that can cause you both harm in the future.

This same dynamic may occur when you tell your best friend or family member about your marriage problems. Now that friend is going to feel uncomfortable around your spouse and may never see them the same way again. It is important to get things off your chest to someone who is sworn to confidentiality and can give you advice as a trained professional.

Ryan didn't realize he opened the door to an affair when he began having frequent conversations with a woman at work. It is through conversations that we build relationships. The lack of conversation in marriage makes you both vulnerable to conversing with others outside the marriage. Ryan's entertaining another woman exponentially worsened his marriage. In fact, his marriage was now on the brink of divorce. While her trust in him had been challenged by his pornography problem, now for sure, there was no more credibility in their marriage. Tiffany's fear that Ryan's "virtual cheating" with other women would lead to his cheating in person was fulfilled. His credibility with himself and Tiffany was greatly damaged. Their agreement to be with no other was now broken. Marriage is built on trust. Without trust – there is no marriage. When credibility diminishes, the two are no longer one. They may live under the same roof, but just like Ryan and Tiffany, they find themselves simply going through the motions. Infidelity feels like a mortal wound in the marriage. It is the most egregious way to hurt your spouse.

Be encouraged to know that like Ryan and Tiffany, many marriages survive infidelity. But their story highlights how important it is to talk through your conflict with each other or a professional rather than with someone outside the sacred marital circle. Tiffany and Ryan villainized each other rather than listening effectively to hear what each other was needing. Ryan was needing his "me" time and Tiffany was need "together" time. They both made the mistake so many couples do, they campaigned to get the other see it their way instead of listening to each other and working things out. Eventually, this led to both seeking solace in someone they perceived as an ally who would support their case against the other. Or, in Ryan's case, would provide some positive energy to get his ego needs met. Tiffany made the mistake of trying to change Ryan's distraction from her using a manipulative approach. She thought she could get his attention by arguing her point, enticing him with lingerie, and begging him to go to bed when she was ready to go to bed. Ryan resisted all her urgings because Tiffany had not reached his heart. If she had listened to him, she *may* have been able to meet his need and prevent him from straying. Ryan made the mistake of trying to change Tiffany's controlling behavior. He used manipulative strategies as well. Instead of seeking to understand her frustration, he argued with her and made her out to be a nag. Framing Tiffany this way gave him an excuse to cheat. He could be with someone who gave him that positive sexual energy he couldn't get from Tiffany at the time because she was angry with him.

Your attempts to change your spouse is damaging. It is so important to give people the right to make their own decisions and determine their own destiny. If your spouse doesn't want to be with you or to keep your family intact, don't waste your time trying to convince them to change their mind. Instead, seek to influence them through your prayers and effectively listening. Don't fight with them. Demonstrate good behaviors and healthy boundaries. Work on yourself, and you will work on your marriage. Do the inner work so the outer will work. They will build more credibility with you when they do it on their own terms.

The conflict you are experiencing in your marriage essentially is a conflict of needs. What both of you needed, the other refuses to give because their needs are not being met. Figuring out what those needs are and how to coordinate the transition to getting those needs met can be a complicated and complex process. You can make this transition yourselves. However, you may desire to seek professional intervention to successfully navigate the many pitfalls in the process and to achieve a positive outcome in the shortest amount of time. Getting professional help as soon as thoughts of separation or divorce arise reduces the chance of even more damage occurring during this stage of marital conflict and disconnection.

For many couples, trust has been so damaged that there is little confidence their partner can change to ever meet their needs. There is a question, especially in the case of abuse or infidelity, whether there is any love there at all. To rebuild trust, it is important for both of you to put energy toward rebuilding your marriage. When both of you are giving your marriage the positive attention it needs it increases your confidence in your marriage. Couples who shift to refocus on their marriage neutralize defeated perceptions and position themselves for success. Couples who are determined to turn things around seek professional help, investing the time, energy, and financial resources necessary to achieve the personal and interpersonal transformation they desire.

You build instant credibility with your partner when you commit to working on yourself to become a better partner in your marriage. When you take personal responsibility for fixing your marriage you can begin the process of healing your credibility. When you acknowledge, account for, and apologize for your bad behavior in this marriage and how you have hurt your spouse, you will begin the healing process.

Too often pride prevents an honest admission of fault. Selfishness gets in the way of forgiveness and grace. Get out of other people's heads and think for yourself. Do you really want to start over again without really trying to fix what you have? Why not address your issues so you won't have to face them again in the next relationship?

REFLECTION

On a scale of 1 to 10, 10 being the highest, how confident are you in your spouse keeping your agreements?

On a scale of 1 to 10, 10 being the highest, how confident is your spouse in your ability to keep your agreements?

Recommit to rebuilding credibility with your spouse and in yourself today. Here are the two mindset shifts you will need to make in order to rebuild credibility. You must **be hopeful** about your ability to meet each other's needs and **be committed** to working on yourself and your marriage.

BE HOPEFUL

Remember the first time when you felt that flutter in your heart for your spouse? I remember when Claudia was organizing my desk at my office when I felt that flutter for the first time. Whether you felt that flutter in your heart or just felt extremely curious, that is when hope began in your relationship. When interest in each other was expressed, hope grew. Hope grew as verbal and physical offers of love were reciprocated. When you finally "fall in love" hope is at an all-time high. As hope builds credibility builds. Each of you needs to feel desired by the other to maintain hope that your relationship can be worthwhile. As agreements are kept hope builds.

Too many jeopardize building credibility and hope by opting to live together instead of getting married. Whether intended or not, this reluctance to commit suggests that credibility is compromised. When a partner perceives the other doesn't like them, is frustrated with them, isn't satisfied with them, or looks down upon them, discouragement sets in.Discouragement depletes hope that this marriage will ever meet one's needs. This is when divorce gets tossed around. When you feel hurt over an extended period of time you can begin to feel hopeless. Hope is triggered when one partner sees the other partner positioning themselves to reinvest in making them happy. Hope is triggered when couples remember what brought them together in the first place in place of unleashing all of that negative energy.

If you feel hopeless about your marriage, it is important to seek professional help. A marriage therapist can help you understand the root of the problem and provide guidance on how to resolve it. With time, effort, and patience, you can build hope in your marriage and create a stronger foundation for the future. Couples should agree to be understanding and respectful of each other and to work together to resolve conflicts. They should also make time for each other and commit to communicating effectively. It is important to keep in mind that marriage is a commitment that requires effort from both partners. By making agreements and working together, couples can keep their marriage strong and enjoy all of the benefits it has to offer!.

When Ryan asked Tiffany to go to therapy with him, even though she was a little anxious about the idea, it made her feel desired by her husband. Going to therapy represents giving your partner a chance. You are saying you still find value in your marriage. For Tiffany to consent to do therapy with Ryan meant to Ryan that he had some influence upon her and she was willing to address her control issues. It is important to your spouse that you acknowledge your behaviors that are causing your spouse stress and frustration. You may have a good reason for those behaviors based on their behaviors. However, taking responsibility for your bad behaviors makes your spouse feel hope for the future. If you are unwilling to address what they perceive as issues, they will be discouraged and not so motivated to work on their issues.

When you step back and look at the big picture, you see how you are impacting each other. Tiffany's controlling behavior caused Ryan to feel claustrophobic and was his justification for reaching out to another woman. Ryan's lying about his pornography caused Tiffany to feel insecure and gave her reason to question his every move. These relationship dynamics are easily overlooked when couples are blaming each other for their problems. A marriage therapist will help you identify your relationship dynamics that are not so easy to see. Understanding the idea that marital relationships are dynamic requires you to expand your thinking beyond what you can feel with your heart, see with your eyes, hear with your ears, or touch with your hands.

Understanding relationship dynamics means putting yourself in your spouse's shoes, feeling what they feel, and seeing things from their perspective. It is recognizing the impact of outside influences on you and your partner. It is listening to them when they tell you how you made them feel and accepting how they feel without you justifying your behavior or sharing how you don't see it that way. It is being sensitive to your partner's feelings and humanity.

Becoming aware of your relationship dynamics makes it easier to take responsibility for your part in the relationship problems and will give both of you hope for resolving your problems.

Too many times couples feel their marriage is hopeless when it can be repaired. Even after couples enter therapy one partner may remain pessimistic about the future of their marriage. This pessimism works against the positive force of therapy. If you have come to believe there is no hope for your marriage, it is difficult to reinvest in the marriage. But if you are going to do therapy, shouldn't you believe it will work?

Many times I've had to help the pessimistic partner realize that being in therapy is the difference maker for their marriage. Having a therapist is an additional resource for your marriage. Therapy changes things. Both of you now have an advocate who is helping you fight for your marriage. Your therapist is your unbiased third party helping both of you see yourselves and guiding you to see things differently so you can behave differently.

Ryan sensed that Tiffany's insecurities created an unhealthy dependence upon him. It was difficult to articulate this to her but having a therapist to analyze and translate was a needed resource for the marriage. Because of Tiffany's dependence issues, it was almost impossible for Ryan to hear her telling him that she needed more time with him. He perceived her bids for his attention as more evidence of her insecurity. Having a therapist translate for Tiffany, Ryan was able to receive the message that if he spent more time with her, she would be less clingy. Getting professional help for your marriage is essential to restoring hope in your marriage'ssuccess.

The idea of divorce for many represents the hope of being relieved from the stress and frustration of their marriage. This neglects the idea that marriage has different stages and phases. One of those phases is acceptance. Wecome into marriage in the stage of blossoming expectations of how this marriage will be so satisfying. Another stage of marriage is fighting over this vision for the marriage. Then finally you come to a stage where you accept it for what it is and stop fighting. After this stage, you begin to see the beauty of your relationship and sense its value in your life. This is a sweet spot many couples fail to achieve because they give up without accessing the resources of those who can help them get through these tough spots Maybe instead of hoping to never have to deal with this person again you can hope to one day have a mutual appreciation for each other.

When two people come together, they bring their own experiences and perspectives. This is both a blessing and a challenge — stronger marriages are built on understanding how each person's history affects their marriage and benefits their union. Unfortunately, marriage difficulties often stem from the baggage we bring into marriage. Whether it be pain or fear from past relationships, unresolved issues with parents, or just a general lack of understanding, self-confidence, or social intelligence, all of us have beenwounded and shaped by negative experiences that bring baggage into our relationships.

The key to dealing with marriage difficulties is learning how to address them together. Couples must be willing to be honest and open about their struggles, listen to each other's perspectives, and work together towards a resolution. This may require therapy, marriage education classes, or even justquality time communicating and having meaningful conversations. The benefits of addressing marriage difficulties together are numerous. A strong marriage provides couples with a secure base from which to grow, develop and explore the world around them. Marriage can be a source of healing for both people, allowing each partner to become a better person and experience greater joy in life. Marriage is an important union that should be valued and nurtured. It takes effort to keep a marriage strong, but the rewards are worth it. By addressing marriage difficulties together and being honest with each other, couples can build more hope in their marriage. They can create a foundation for a strong marriage that will last through time.

Keep hope alive in your marriage knowing that if you keep fighting for your marriage, you will one day succeed in creating that marriage you have always wanted to be in.

REFLECTION

On a scale of 1 to 10, 10 being the highest, how confident are you in your ability to meet your partner's needs?

On a scale of 1 to 10, 10 being the highest, how hopeful are you that your partner can meet your needs?

BE COMMITTED

With hope comes a commitment to fulfill the agreements and live life together. Commitment is the motivation to keep moving toward each other. Commitment is what it takes to make it through the ups and downs of life.

Commitment is what it takes to deal with temporary duty, layoffs, sick crying babies in the middle of the night, and absolute failures like infidelity.

But everybody's commitment level is different. Some people are hard workers and not easily discouraged when they make their minds up about something. Others give up easily when facing resistance. The circumstances upon which you got married play a significant impact on your commitment level. If you got married because you were pregnant and wanted to do the "right" thing vs. I couldn't wait to be Mr. & Mrs., there may be a distinct difference in your commitment level. It is very important to have very little doubt when choosing a spouse.

Ryan and Tiffany didn't feel coerced to get married. They were truly in love with each other and believed they were making an excellent choice. Their love had built over time once interest was registered. However, their long-distance relationship leading up to marriage put a strain on the development of their relationship. They really weren't able to spend a lot of time together before marriage. So, once they married, they were finally getting to know each other. The more time they spent together the more they began to clash over this and that. Because of their poor communication skills, these clashes went unresolved and turned into resentment. Before long, they were no longer enjoying their marriage and wondered if they had made a mistake. It seems it doesn't matter how long you date or even if you live together, once married you will more than likely experience these clashes. Couples who work on their communication skills are always much better able to work through these differences. Taking the time before you get married to work on these skills in premarital counseling is strongly advised.

In order to build commitment, your marriage must have apurpose. For most people, the essential purpose of marriage is being able to enjoy a satisfying companionship and feeling loved, desired, and appreciated. Each of you needs to feel desired by the other. When a spouse perceives the other doesn't like them, is frustrated with them, or is looked down upon, discouragement sets in. Discouragement is a loss of hope that this marriage will ever meet one's needs. This is when divorce gets tossed around. Hope is triggered when one partner sees the other partner positioning themselves toreinvest in making them happy. Hope is triggered when couples remember what brought them together in the first place.

Marriage is complicated. There are many moving parts to keep up with. There's you, me, us, and everybody else. There are so many pitfalls to avoid and obstacles to climb. It is so easy for time to pass while a couple is out of sync. What was once a fiery exciting relationship can become a bore. There is so much that goes into a successful relationship. It seems like there are so many forces in play to tear you apart and create distance between you. Because life is full of seasons it is almost inevitable for a couple to experience busy seasons when the marriage is neglected. Couples drift apart during these seasons naturally. But a couple must continually refocus on their relationship to keep the flame of love flaming.A couple must stay in touch to keep the marriage *Sizzling Hot*.It is critical for couples to stay open to each other along life's journey.

My wife and I didn't get a chance to enjoy an extended version of the warm fuzzy of the newlywed experience because we started with a lot going on. We were a blended family. Having at least nine months to prepare for a child is a serious blessing. For us, we had no time to get to know one another without kids. It was a rough transition. In fact, almost 20 years later, we are still dealing with blended family issues.

Yet, while this journey hasn't been without stumbles and disappointments, it has been a steady climb upward. We've learned along the way how to keep things steamy. Despite all the challenges, God has blessed us to keep a steady line of communication open and opportunities to keep refocusing on our relationship. While we would never claim to be a model couple, we have learned how to stay in touch. We really have a simple relationship embedded in living life together. We could do more weekend rendezvous and engage in a more rigorous dating routine. Because of our imperfections, we are still learning how to manage our time. We have learned, though, to keep the conversation going between us. We got together in the first place because we liked talking to each other. This conversation has kept our connection strong. This conversation helps us to remember our vows to "have and to hold from this day forward, for better, for worse, for richer, for poorer, in sickness and health, until death do us part."

The marriage vow represents the connection a couple must maintain through the ups and downs of life. This connection can only be maintained when couples make their marital relationship a priority and something they stay committed to.

You may be in one of those busy or dry seasons of life, headed into one, or coming out of one. If you are going to keep the sizzle (or get it back), you must have a *Sizzle Mindset*. Don't throw out your icebox. Work on heating things up. After facing conflict, distance and trouble you must be determined to *Return to Love* one another. Romans 12:10 NIV says "Be devoted to one another in love. Honor one another above yourselves." Ecclesiastes 9:9 NIV says "Enjoy life with your wife, whom you love, all the days of this meaningless life that God has given you under the sun—all your meaningless days. For this is your lot in life and in your toilsome labor under the sun." Ephesians 4:32 NKJV says "And be kind to one another, tenderhearted, forgiving one another, even as God in Christ forgave you."

Scripture always points us in the right direction. The enemy wants to separate us–God wants to bring us together. A *Sizzle Mindset* is when you keep love on your mind. You keep coming back to *Return to Love*. That is how you keep the passion alive in your marriage. You must remember the vow you made to love one another–till death do us part.

The secret to having a *Sizzle Mindset* is to remember your "I do's". It is so easy to get discouraged when things are not going the way you want them to. Especially for extended periods of time. Forgetting the commitment you made for life, however long ago, is a death sentence for your marriage. You can't stay married if you are not committed to your marriage.

Marriage is difficult. Did you expect it to be a cakewalk when you said I DO? So, you've got to draw on your 'till death do us part' commitment during those dry seasons. Let me tell you–there will be some dry seasons. It will be your commitment that will keep you energized to keep coming back and working on your marriage.

A friend of mine shared how he realized he and his wife had really gotten out of sync after his last child went off to college. The house was quiet. He and his wife were not having very many conversations. They had forgotten about each other having been so busy raising their children. This was a dry season for them. He told me that he flirted with the idea of divorce but couldn't convince himself to do it when he remembered his vow– 'for better or for worse'. He said that he decided to take his wife on a romantic vacation to Greece and it was just what they needed to reignite the flame. Remembering his vows gave him the energy and creativity to reinvest in his marriage.

It is sad when two hearts that were once bound in love turn cold and hardened toward each other. Some of the worse fights you will see are two once-lovers fighting over the custody of their child. The enemy has done this. But it is an awesome thing when God turns things around. God brings peace and Harmony. The devil brings strife and division. You must protect your marriage from the devil.

Where the Spirit of the Lord is, there is freedom from strife and division. (2 Corinthians 3:17) So it stands to reason thatwhere the spirit of Satan is there is bondage–where love is restricted and restrained.

I had a young man return to my office a year and a half later to tell me the story of how the Lord turned his and his wife's hearts back toward one another. "It was a miracle," he exclaimed. In another situation, a couple shared how one thing after another blocked their attempts to even file their divorce paperwork. Somehow, some way God used that time to cause them to *Return to Love* and restore their unity. God can change your heart toward your spouse. However, you must become open to seeing your spouse differently. God changed my perspective toward my wife when I turned to him asking for help. He revealed to me that I didn't love her. He changed me from being so concerned about what she wasn'tdoing for me to what I wasn't doing for her. I was so concerned about how she was making me feel rather than taking responsibility for my own feelings. Instead of focusing on her behavior I began to focus on improving my behavior. A changed perspective leads to changed feelings, and changed feelings lead to changed behaviors.

Is it possible that the angle from which you are looking at something affects your judgment of what you are looking at? I've noticed a common trait many struggling couples share - the inability to consider the other person's perspective. It's like they can only see yellow. And yellow is the way they see things. They can't see blue, green, or red - what others can see. This can be the most challenging obstacle to overcome in the marital relationship and in the therapy room. If you find yourself frequently saying "I disagree" or "you're lying", you probably can only see yellow. Stop taking responsibility for what everybody else thinks, feels, and does. Let them have their perspective. Listen and learn from them. It has made the world of difference in my marriage. I can now see yellow, blue, green, and red.

Consider why you chose your partner in the first place. Remember why you took those vows. Don't allow anything to eclipse the love that you started with. From what perspective were you looking at them then? If your marriage is lacking sizzle, then the perspective from which you viewed your spouse has shifted. You are not seeing them in the positive light you once did. Perhaps their value to you has declined because some expectations haven't been met. Possibly they have disappointed you in several ways. If you want to get the sizzleback, you must change your perspective of your spouse. You must focus on their positive attributes. You may not be able to return to your original view of them, but you can begin focusing on some of their positives rather than their negatives. This is what a *Sizzle Mindset* will do for you. It will help you look past their faults to see their good. It helps you focus on how you are doing rather than what they are doing.

If you have lost your sizzle–you must challenge yourself to stop looking at what annoys you and start looking at what you appreciate about your mate. You must shift to focusing on becoming a better spouse yourself. I have found that the essence of why a couple chooses one another never leaves. They may be arguing like cats and dogs and may seem to be destined for divorce; however, a slightly changed perspective easily leads to an amazingly restored connection. But this is impossible if they are not committed to their marriage. I've helped hundreds of couples get their sizzle back and *Return to Love*. But not one when one or both are no longer committed to their marriage vow.

You may have to revisit your view of marriage as well. It is easy in this humanistic 'it depends' society to justify falling out of love and moving on. But if you see marriage as permanent—something that only an extreme experience could justify ending—you will turn back repeatedly to work on your union. If marriage is disposable, then you see marriage as valuable only when it is convenient and enjoyable. Those who avoid eating their vegetables think vegetables are optional. Their consequence is failure to enjoy the life-giving health benefits of vegetables. Those who see marriage for a time rather than a lifetime fail to receive the full benefits of a lifelong commitment to one person. The way you see marriage affects your words and actions toward your spouse. Your commitment level will determine which way you are moving in your relationship. You are either moving toward your marriage or away from it. Let me encourage you to remember your vows and not allow the enemy to steal what belongs to you.

Here's the bottom line in keeping sizzle in your marriage—you should keep moving toward one another, producing warmth and good feelings. You must make love your priority. That means despite your partner's unattractive actions and words, you should respond in loving ways. What your eyes cannot see, your ears cannot hear, and your heart cannot feel must be dictated by your mind. You must decide to be loving. Because what we do is motivated by what we feel, it is difficult to be loving when you don't feel the love. But throughout a lifetime of marriage, you don't always feel the love. Sometimes you must do loving things from an intellectual perspective.

That's where feelings come from, anyway. You must make up your mind to be loving. You may not see your partner's love, hear any loving words come out of their mouth, or feel any warmth from them, but if you want to keep or restore your sizzle, you must make a conscious decision to *Return to Love*. This comes from remembering your vows, remembering what you once had or what you hope to have, and becoming the person you want your spouse to be. This new loving behavior has the power to change your heart and the heart of your spouse. A new perspective! Love is hard to resist.

Do you remember why you married your spouse? It doesn't take us much to forget things. It never ceases to amaze me how difficult it is for us to remember what big things we accomplished last year. We are constantly looking forward to what still needs to be accomplished. We forget so easily. A series of events and experiences over time can effectively change how you see your spouse and marriage altogether. In fact, the same thing you loved about them at one time can become what you can't stand about them later. If you are going to keep a *Sizzle Mindset*, you mus remember what you value in your spouse. You should remember what you fell in love with. You need to remember the vows you made. Recall the vows you made on your wedding day and recommit to your betrothed. This is the secret to heating things up so you don't have to throw out your icebox. This is how you keep the passion alive in your marriage.

REFLECTION

On a scale of 1 to 10, 10 being the highest, how confident are you in your commitment to your marital relationship?

On a scale of 1 to 10, 10 being the highest, how confident are you in your spouse's commitment to your marital relationship?

CHAPTER FIVE
Confirmation

BE FLEXIBLE & BE AVAILABLE

Do you remember being a child passing notes saying, "I like you!" "Do you like me?" Didn't you get excited when they said yes or depressed when they had the nerve to say no?

Confirmation is confirming and affirming your belief in, love for, and commitment to your spouse. It is effectively communicating "I love you" in word and deed. Confirmation is built with conversation, admiration, affection, and lovemaking. Confirmation is destroyed with the silent treatment, name-calling, and criticizing. Confirmation is letting your spouse know that you still love them, and that you still have their back.

Confirmation is a term used in psychology to refer to the process of verifying that a statement is true. In marriage, confirmation is important to ensure that both partners are on the same page and that any issues that arise can be addressed quickly and effectively. In order to confirm marriage issues, it is necessary for couples to talk openly and honestly with each other about how they feel. This allows them to work through any disagreements they may have and come to a resolution. Confirmation also helps couples to feel secure in their marriage, as they know that they can trust each other. Confirming your love in marriage isn't always easy, but it is necessary for a marriage to be successful and thrive. It is especially difficult when you are at odds with one another. If you can feel hurt or disappointed yet are able to express your love and appreciation for your spouse during a disagreement, you will enjoy a more peaceful and productive resolution of problems.

It is natural for us to seek a primary attachment to another adult who will provide mutual support for our social, emotional, psychological, and physical needs. Companionship is an inherent adult human need. We need someone who can say we are worthwhile when we make mistakes or get beat up by life. We need a safe retreat from the world to recharge and recreate. When mutual confirmation fails, we begin looking outside of the relationship for ways to get confirmation and risk forming inappropriate relationships with another lover, work, a hobby, family, friends, or even children.

This is what happened to Ryan and Tiffany. Over time as couples experience unresolved conflict, they pull away from each other. They stop confirming their love for each other with displays of love, affection, and respect. They begin to look to others for confirmation. Hope is triggered when couples begin to show each other love again. Once couples commit to working on their marriage, they begin to reconsider what it was about each other that they fell in love with and begin to do those things that drew them to each other initially. Couples must rediscover their original dream for their relationship and begin again confirming their love for each other by restoring the affection, time together, and activities they used to do together.

Ryan and Tiffany loved the Lord and really enjoyed reading and discussing the Bible together. When Ryan first prayed with her, Tiffany knew he was 'The one.' She never had a boyfriend who was as spiritually inclined as Ryan. This melted her heart. This spiritual connection was at the heart of what confirmed their love. At the height of their conflict, they stopped studying and praying together as much. What drew them together they were no longer doing. Now they were not sure if they were meant for each other.

Do you remember what clinched it for you that this was 'The one?' After going through a divorce, I was determined to pick better next time. So, I made a list of what I believe I should be looking for in a woman. I remember checking off most of those items with Claudia. It was then that I realized I had found 'The one.' Essentially, I was looking for someone who shared my values. Someone I could serve alongside. Working together in ministry to others is something we do well together. When we are doing a big dinner, we are in our element. Hospitality is our superpower as a couple. During the dips in our marriage, I try to remember how good we are together.

When you are heavily engaged in conflict, it is unlikely you are working optimally as the dynamic duo you were meant to be. At the height of my conflict with Claudia, we found ourselves arguing in the kitchen in front of our guests. How embarrassing. It was during this time that I questioned whether we should be together. Conflict is de-confirming. It brings out the worse in us. You must make adjustments to your thinking if you are going to turn things around. That starts with being more flexible and making yourself more available.

Claudia and I are both leaders with strong opinions about how things should go. In the earlier stages of our marriage I would go toe to toe with her. As I matured, I became more flexible and available. This gave her more security and confirmed my love for her. Over time, she has become more flexible and available. Confirmation is built by being flexible and available.

BE FLEXIBLE

Stretching is a very important exercise to remember. There have been several times I failed to do so prior to exercise and paid the price for it. Failure to stretch limits your range of motion and makes you more prone to injury. And what you don't use you eventually lose. This same principle applies to marriage. Living with another person requires stretching. We must stretch our perspective to allow for someone else's. We must stretch our plans to include someone else's plans. Failure to stretch severely limits the relationship's growth. And our personal growth as well. Too many people stay in their bubble (comfort zone) and fail to learn and achieve new things in their lives. Marriage is a great opportunity for self-actualization. But too often we get stuck in thinking our way is the only way and fail to receive what our spouse is offering.

Flexibility is making your spouse's needs your priority. Up to this point, decisions have been made regardless of your spouse. Justifications for bad behavior are given blaming the other. In order to restore the marriage, couples must make adjustments in their time and priorities. They must learn how to listen to each other to understand and stop judging each other negatively. They must be open to doing things differently.

I honestly used to think it was my job to make my wife happy. I didn't realize that it was her job to find happiness—mine to treat her like a queen. But I didn't know that in the early days of our marriage. I would take the time to give her my wonderful ideas about how I thought she should think about things, how she should say things, how she should get over things, etc. And yes, many times these sharing times turned into heated arguments because she didn't quite see it as I did.

Ultimately God showed me that the way I was going about things was not the way he wanted me to love my wife. I learned the lecture/argue/debate method is not loving my wife. You're not showing love when you are trying to change your spouse. In fact, trying to change your spouse sends a strong message to your spouse that they are not good enough for you as they are. If you are sending those negative messages, what messages do you expect to get in return?

Loving someone is accepting them for who they are. Loving someone is accepting their faults. Loving someone is loving them despite their faults. Love overlooks faults (1 Peter 4:8) not put them on blast on social media. If the two of you have gotten into the cycle of declaring one another's faults you have made no room for faults. If you make no room for faults, you are in trouble – because we all have faults. If faults become your focus, you become very inflexible and unloving.

Your relationship becomes a very dark place when all you can see are one another's faults.

It was 10 years into our marriage when Mr. Fixit finally learned to lay off the hammer and chisel. It was when I put them away that I finally could see the beauty in my wife that I hadn't seen in a long time. When I no longer judged her, I could see her for the wonderful woman she is. When I no longer expected her to be a mini-me I could finally see what I originally saw when I picked her out. With this different perspective of my wife, I was finally able to connect with her. I had finally become flexible enough to allow her world. I was no longer stuck on my opinion. I had opened up to allow her to have her own perspective. I was willing to allow her to be wrong according to me and right according to her. This is another great secret of staying connected and maintaining a *Sizzling Hot Marriage.*

Another way to look at it is by choosing your battles. If you want to keep your marriage sizzling, you must limit the conflict and contention between you. If you make a big deal out of every little thing and think your spouse needs your feedback constantly, the sizzle will quickly disappear. Some things are just not that important - that includes your idea about how things should go. The differences we face in our relationship range from small to big to huge. Most of the things we face are small things that we often make huge. At the end of the day, they are insignificant matters of opinion that amount only to how you slice the cake. Everybody has a different method of slicing. Couples get into huge arguments trying to decide which way is the "right way" to slice it. If you are going to maintain a *Sizzling Hot Marriage*, you must determine to be flexible when it comes to insignificant things.

The other day my wife called me on her way home from work complaining about what had happened that day. Before I knew it, I caught myself trying to help her "think right". I had taken out my hammer and chisel. I realized what I had done when I started feeling frustrated. In those situations, those anxious unsettled feelings are always my signal that I'm trying to force-feed my version of what's right to someone else. I used to blame her for those feelings. But now I recognize that I'm the culprit. Now I can do something about the problem instead of depending on her to make me feel better. By taking responsibility for my emotions, I have freed Claudia from my oppression.

Whereas before, I was hopelessly and helplessly dependent on her changing her attitude before I could change mine. Now I immediately shut my mouth to listen to her and appreciate her perspective. Well, most of the time. Yes, I would have handled the situation differently than she did. But I'm not her. She deserves her own successes and failures in life. Who says I'm the all-knowing one anyway? This is the flexibility that is essential in marriage.

So many fail to be flexible enough to listen. Everything they hear they judge and have determined that everyone else's judgment is inferior to theirs. They must have the last word and can only speak from their perspective. Some people make everything about themselves and rarely if ever share the floor with others. Couples must remember that there are two brains in their marriage. Both brains are individually capable of making independent judgments. Remember there are a dozen ways to do one task. Couples must learn how to share the floor, how to be flexible, and not have to have one's way all the time. This is the *Sizzle Mindset*.

Learning how to mind my own business and allowing my wife to mind her own business has been a huge blessing for us. No longer responsible for her happiness and success in life, I can now fully focus on being her support cast while I put the majority of my energy on my happiness and success in life.

Truthfully, I was stressing my wife out. Ask her. She'll tell you. Since I realized what was my responsibility, I have tried to leave my wife's faults alone. Even when her fault is reminding me of my faults. Certainly, as I shared above, I have my moments of picking up my hammer and chisel. The secret is to be aware when your frustration is rising and quickly put them back into the tool bag where they belong.

The way to change your spouse is to love them. Jesus didn't come to condemn the world but to love the world. (John 3:17) He said if I be lifted up I will draw all men to me. (John 12:32) If you are irritated, frustrated, and unnerved with your spouse, you have somehow slipped into a role that you don't belong. This applies to everybody else in your life too. The secret to a happy *Sizzling Hot Marriage* is to live and let live. Give your spouse the space to be stuck on stupid. Recognize that their living with you is not a cakewalk. Stop trying to do and be everything in your marriage. Do your part. Focus on your job. Not helping them do theirs. The greatest sermon ever preached is the one lived. Stop being a hypocrite. Shut your mouth, stop talking about it and be about it. You may have bumped into a fault of your spouse that is big. Their fault is causing problems for you. How you handle that fault has a direct impact on whether that fault increases or decreases in size. Becoming your spouse's parent constantly instructing, yelling, and chastising them for their fault is not going to have the impact you hope. That behavior will only drive a deeper wedge between you. Learn to pray for your spouse. God will reveal to you what to say and when to say it. Remember these two things. If you have a problem and need wisdom to solve it, ask God for wisdom. (James 1:5) if you seek God first, all these things will be added to you. (Matthew7:7) You don't have to pester and worry your spouse. Trust that God will make things right in His time.

Prayer is certainly your most powerful tool for change.

Pray for those who use you and mistreat you. (Matthew 5:44) Watch them change. Don't return evil for evil. (Romans 12:17) Return good for evil. Smile when they frown. Laugh when they yell. Give words of encouragement when they are spewing hatred. Be who you are wanting them to be. Mind your own business and allow God to develop them in the areas in which they are weak. Be flexible–this is what it takes to confirm your love and keep the sizzle in your marriage. In fact,

God is working on you to be more flexible. Maybe that is why He gave you your spouse.

Ryan recognized that he hadn't been very flexible with Tiffany. Now that she had forgiven him for his infidelity, he seemed to have a lot more space in his heart for her perspective. He was humbled that she was giving him a second chance. There is no doubt that Tiffany was being flexible with Ryan. She was hurt and disappointed by what he had done. But she loved him and was willing to forgive him.

She believed in him and was committed to working on their marriage. She also realized that her inflexibility had played a part in driving him away. She was determined to do better.

BE AVAILABLE

When conflict arises in marriage couples explode and withdraw. These explosions can be loud or silent. Explosions and withdrawals eat away at the marital bond. Once an opinion is formed there is nothing the other can say to change it. Couples argue about any and everything. Couples find themselves on separate sides of every issue and of the house. They begin to live life independently and are just roommates. They are just going through the motions acting married, but they are separated emotionally, spiritually, and physically. In order to turn things around there must be a mindset shift to open back up to each other and see each other as a person again. Your spouse is not your enemy. Couples must be open to spending more time together, hearing what each other has to say and responding positively to what each other has to say.

In case after case, the central problem that lands couples in my office is their failure to spend time together.

You liked this person enough to marry them and you declared your undying love. But over time you began focusing on other things. Maybe you had children and began to focus on them. Maybe work got busy or you had to focus on aging parent issues. Maybe conflict came between you. Maybe some things happened that got you off track. Whatever may have happened you have a choice about what you will do from this day forward. The second mindset shift you can make to confirm your love is being more available to your spouse. Availability is taking time out for your marriage.

Life is full of choices. You can easily dig your head in the sand and forget all about your spouse. You can get too busy, and your time together disappears. Without sufficient time together, inevitably you will stop seeing your spouse as your partner and see them as someone causing you problems. Your partner's flaws will begin to outweigh your companionship. The more time you spend together the more you can grow to understand each other and become more compassionate toward one another. The more time you spend together the more memories you will make. The more time you spend together the less you will see each other's flaws. When you don't spend time together you may find yourselves no longer liking each other. Most couples who show up for counseling share that they spend very little to no time together. What does that tell you? Remember practice perfects. What you do repeatedly you will naturally become better at. The more time you spend together the better you will become at getting along and enjoying your relationship. The better you will become at loving each other. The contrary is true as well, the less time you spend together, the more important those other things will become to you. The less "in love" you will feel.

The value you get from your marriage is the companionship that you signed up for in the first place. You got married for companionship. If you want a better marriage, take more initiative to spend more time together. Revive your companionship and you will revive your relationship. Making time to be available to spend with your spouse is the *Sizzle Mindset*. You are making love your priority. And time is love.

If you want a *Sizzle Mindset* or want to get the sizzle back in your marriage you must spend at least five hours of undivided attention time together each week. No TV, cell phone, or other people. Just the two of you spending time engaging with each other. Couples who rarely make it to my office are getting the equivalent of two hours together each day -14 hours each week. That's about 8% of your entire week. When you think about it, isn't that what you signed up for? To be together.

Spending less time than this places your marriage in jeopardy of becoming insignificant to you. Spending this amount of time together may require a perspective change. Is it possible that you have invested too much time in other things and other people? You must be intentional about your face time with your spouse. You must adjust your schedule to ensure you get time to peer into one another's eyes. You must remove distractions and devices to enjoy each other's undivided attention. When will you spend time together?

Movies and TV don't count for undivided attention. The movie is your focus of attention. You may be spending time together, but you are not looking at each other. You must talk to each other looking into each other's eyes if you want to rekindle the fire. Most people begin their relationship talking and find a significant level of satisfaction in communicating with each other. By doing so you confirm you love and desire for each other.

There is often a difference between "before marriage" and "after marriage" communication. Before marriage, the conversation can be shallow and pretentious but very warm and cozy. The whole idea of courting is presenting your best side and hiding your bad side. Because we often come to the mating table severely insecure and fearing rejection, we are thinking more about our impression than about revealing our most personal vulnerabilities. Thus, we focus on impressing our potential suitor rather than being our authentic selves. Thus, our conversations can potentially never reveal who we really are.

After marriage, you let down your hair and the real you is revealed; and it is often after marriage that all your personal problems are manifested. So many couples are shocked to face something totally different from what they experienced prior to marriage–even if they lived together. Bewildered, they eventually find themselves in separate corners in retreat from the fiery dissension and tension.

Many couples find themselves enduring months of silent treatment. To get the sizzle back one of you must break the ice, and the other one must reciprocate. The way to come up with ideas about things to do together. Ask your spouse out on a date. Buy a conversation game. Let your spouse know you are interested in spending time with them. Many sins can be forgiven when you restore your companionship. The time together will revive your companionship as you make new memories that will outrank the old. We can't do anything about the past. It is so important to live in the present. The past is gone–why focus on it? Today is what many couples fail to focus on. Tomorrow is not promised–why be afraid of it? Enjoy today and make your tomorrow great! Make the best of today so you can have a bright tomorrow.

I realized, in retrospect, that the intense conflict I was experiencing with Claudia was during a time when I would see clients from eight in the morning till eight in the evening. Inadvertently I had placed the stress of the home and kids on her. I wasn't spending time with her or the kids. We had big arguments over this. But I thought I was doing what I needed to do. She would tell me I was in control of my schedule. And I would say I wasn't. Well, who was correct?

I wasn't physically available, and I wasn't emotionally available. When I was home, I checked a lot of things off the list including putting the babies to bed, having worship, getting them up and out to school, washing and folding clothes, etc. I couldn't understand why she wasn't happy with me. There was one thing I failed to add to my list – relationship building time together with her and with the children. But nothing she was saying was entering my consciousness. I was stuck in my own perspective. I know now, I was the reason we had all those arguments I blamed her for.

As I reflect on my first marriage, I don't recall a lot of arguing. But I know I was even more headstrong then. Here are the consequences not paying attention to the emotional needs of your spouse – they will withdraw from you and may leave you altogether. I know there were many other factors that contributed to our divorce, but I can't help but believe I was the same guy checking off lists but forgetting the most important currency of relationships – time together.

Ryan realized that he hadn't made space in his life for Tiffany. He thought he could carry his habits into his marriage without making any adjustments. Tiffany had tried to let him know that he needed to be more balanced, but Ryan interpreted her as being controlling. Now he sees that he should have listened. Now he is making more effort to spend time with her and make it clear that she is his priority. This has made Tiffany feels so much more secure in their marriage. Ryan has realized that his life is fuller now that he has moved his personal agenda to the side to focus more on spending time with Tiffany. He is making her his favorite activity.

What do you want to do with your spouse? What has your spouse been begging you to do? Go do it! What is holding you back? Don't let the tension, disappointment or anger get in the way. Get your calendar out today and start making plans to spend time together. When something comes up that gets in the way of your plans ensure that you make up for it. If you want to keep the sizzle in your marriage, you should develop a more active dating and time-together lifestyle. A *Sizzle Mindset* returns to love and makes time for love. Keep the passion alive in your marriage by being available.

REFLECTION

On a scale of 1 to 10, 10 being the highest, how well do you confirm your love for your spouse?

On a scale of 1 to 10, 10 being the highest, how well does your spouse confirm their love for you?

CHAPTER SIX
Compassion

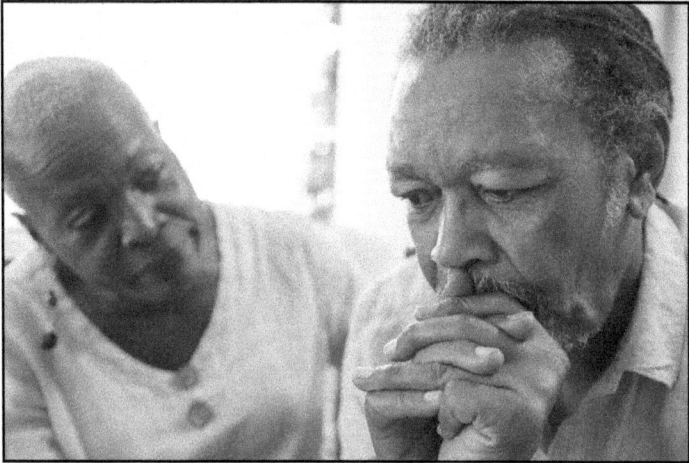

BE CALM

Compassion is awareness of others' distress coupled with the desire to alleviate it. It is the tenderness we seek to experience in a loving relationship. It is built by being aware of and meeting the basic needs of your spouse. It is destroyed by not paying attention to your spouse. Impatience, abuse, and neglect clearly are behaviors that display a lack of compassion.

Conflict breeds contempt. Contempt is a state where couples unashamedly display their disregard for one another. Couples show contempt through sarcasm, interruption, avoidance, silent treatment, passive, passive-aggressive, and aggressive behaviors. Compassion occurs when the couple humanizes each other again. Couples must calm down and create a safe space for intimate conversations. They can do this by attaching more considerate meanings to the behaviors they have tagged as attacking, unloving, and undesirable in each other. They can do this by acknowledging their wrongs to each other. They can do this by forgiving each other. They can do this by seeing beyond their own pain to feel the pain of the other. They can do this by listening to each other rather than judging each other.

Ryan refused to see Tiffany any other way but controlling. In fact, he used this negative descriptor to justify cheating on her. Subconsciously he was saying he deserved to take a break from Tiffany because her controlling behavior was so unbearable. As long as he saw her as the antagonist, he had a way to justify to doing his dirt.

Deception is awful. Self-deception is sad. It is amazing how we find reasons to justify evil. Like stealing something because we have convinced ourselves we must have it and the other person doesn't need it. Ryan had convinced himself he deserved the affections of another woman because the one he had was controlling.

We must remain prayerful. Not one of us is safe from self-deception. The key to escaping the claws of greed, lust, and temptation is compassion. Sin always hurts someone. The thought that no one will get hurt is a lie from the belly of Satan. The other lie is no one will know. The problem with both those justifications is it totally discounts the hurt the sin will bring upon you and conveniently ignores the others who inevitably will be hurt as well.

Ryan's decision to have an affair left the woman with a scar from being used by another man. Ryan's upstanding Christian reputation had been tarnished. Ryan hurt the foundation of his marriage. He destroyed his Credibility as Tiffany could no longer trust his word. He destroyed his Confirmation that he loves Tiffany and has her back. He displayed no Compassion toward Tiffany in the actions he took. His actions disrupted their Community identity as a married couple. Ryan had to now deal with the guilt of his sin and how much hurt he has caused.

Tiffany was now writhing in heartbreak, anxiety, and sadness as she was grieving the loss of the purity of their love. The pain of betrayal is almost unbearable. Tiffany now has the burden of deciding whether she will have compassion for Ryan.

Compassion is feeling a sense of deep sympathy and sorrow for another who is stricken by misfortune, accompanied by a strong desire to alleviate the suffering. In order to have compassion for someone else, you must escape your own sorrow and pain. It seems humanly impossible to show compassion to someone who has hurt you. This is something God has to help you with. He has to give you his comfort and grace to do so.

Tiffany decided that Ryan was sincere in his remorse for what he had done. She realized that his behavior was only indirectly saying he didn't love her. She could understand that his affair was a direct consequence of his view of women as objects of his desire. It was only a matter of time before he would act on his virtual fantasies. When she saw that Ryan saw the connection and apologized for the affair, the porn, and the lies, his credibility grew with her. This all gave her the confidence that showing him compassion (vs. dishing out justice) was the decision she should make. She believed there was a high probability Ryan would never hurt her like this again. Ryan and Tiffany's compassion challenge was major. Most couples have only minor breaches of trust to deal with.

Are you exercising grace and compassion toward your spouse or are you constantly reminding them of their faults?

REFLECTION

On a scale of 1 to 10, 10 being the highest, how compassionate are you toward your spouse?

On a scale of 1 to 10, 10 being the highest, how compassionate is your spouse toward you?

You build compassion when you learn to be calm.

BE CALM

While Ryan and Tiffany didn't yell and become disrespectful when they felt angry with each other, they were not calm. Every day they felt anxious and tense. Because they ended up fighting over every little thing, they were not calm. They were snappy with each other. They were quick to complain and find fault with each other. They were on edge and easily upset with each other. Because they were not happy with each other, any niceness was out of general courtesy. And there was no niceness in their facial expressions. They were in full 'going through the motions' mode. In this state, there were no warm expressions of love. They found themselves at odds with each other. They had built a case against each other and every time the other did something wrong it was further evidence to build their case. This was a full-out war.

Why in the world would being calm reveal compassion in a marital relationship? The condition couples in conflict find themselves in is one of judgment against each other. Each is blaming the other for their misery and suffering. Compassion involves thinking about the needs of the other person. If you are not being calm with someone, you are not thinking about their needs, you are thinking about your needs.

Couples in conflict are going through the grieving process. They are losing their dream for their relationship. They dreamed to live together happily for the rest of their lives together. Now with the tension, they are worrying if their marriage will make it. In this space, they are thinking about their own survival - not each other's needs. Grief involves denial, anger, depression, indecision, and finally acceptance of your loss. Calmness occurs when one comes to the place of accepting their loss. Until you accept what you have lost, you won't position yourself to fix your problem.

The mindset shift required to be calm is acceptance. You must be willing to accept things the way they are, no longer having a need to control the narrative. Because we want what we want when we want it is difficult to accept when we don't get it. This is why we lie, cheat, steal, yell, interrupt, and manipulate others. In addition, we want others to see us favorably all the time no matter what dirty deeds we have done. So, we avoid conversations, change the subject, shut down, get loud, run away, twist things back on the other person, or simply make up a story to paint ourselves in a positive light.

If you are actively working to manage the narrative, you are not calm and are not positioned to show your spouse compassion. You are not able to listen. In this state of mind, all you want to do is talk over your spouse in order to influence them to see it the way you want them to see it. You must learn to accept the truth and deal with it like an adult.

The truth of how your spouse thinks about you might be painful - but it's the truth. You can't fix the problem if you can't settle down and accept your spouse's truth. If you did the crime, you must be willing to do the time.

Despite Ryan's remorse and contrite spirit regarding his stepping out on Tiffany, he had a difficult time dealing with Tiffany when she brought up what he had done. He would get angry with her and say something that blamed her for bringing up the past. This didn't make Tiffany feel like he was taking responsibility for what he had done to the relationship. Or show her any compassion. This was Ryan trying to control the narrative and make it seem like what he had done was done and over. But it wasn't. It takes years for a relationship to heal after infidelity. It takes a year or so of compassionate responses for the injured spouse to significantly reduce brining up what happened. If he wanted that wound to heal, he would apologize to Tiffany and remind her that he loved her every time she brought it up.

Intimidating her to stop bringing it up was not going to keep her from thinking about it. It was just a way to control the narrative.

Each partner must learn to press the easy button instead of the panic button. It requires self-confidence, self-esteem, and self-efficacy. This step often requires some deep inner work resolving unresolved issues from childhood, learning to take responsibility for oneself, learning how to be more aware of one's impact on others' emotions and behaviors, learning how to allow others to be responsible for themselves, and learning how to set up and enforce effective boundaries.

Learning how to make yourself happy contributes to your spouse's happiness. You must shift your mindset to become more aware of yourself and your spouse to become a *Sizzling Hot Marriage.*

You must make the mindset shift to be calm, cool, and collected.

Staying focused on feeling good is a critical component of maintaining a healthy mind, body, and relationship. This is probably the most important chapter in the entire book. I'm going to take some time explaining the importance of feeling good, how to feel good, and how to do what you can to help your spouse feel good. Being happy is an important characteristic of a happy marriage. Knowing how to be happy and managing your anger and other negative emotions is essential to maintaining a *Sizzle Mindset.* Happy people make happy marriages.

Replacing the negativity between you and your spouse with positivity will guarantee a *Sizzling Hot Marriage.* You can't have a happy marriage without happy people.

Happiness is an individual's emotion and is not dependent upon someone else. It is a choice an individual must make. Negative emotions like anger, hurt, frustration, anxiety, and depression are what reduce marital satisfaction. You should not allow the sun to go down on your anger. (Ephesians 4:26) Your negative emotions can indeed get you in trouble. You must learn to be angry without saying mean things or withdrawing from your spouse.

HOW TO MANAGE YOUR EMOTIONS

It is very difficult to see love in angry outbursts. For sinful humans, anger comes from a self-centered perspective.

When you're angry there are some things, you may not be considering. For example, you may be more concerned about letting the anger out rather than how well your message is being received. You may not be thinking enough about the other person as you should. You may lack compassion. When angry you think a lot about yourself. You must remain even-tempered and not become so easily agitated, angered, anxious, or aroused. You must learn how to manage your mood and regulate your emotions. You may have a valid objection to something your spouse said or did. But that doesn't justify your leaving conversational mode and becoming contentious or withdrawn. Adults must be able to speak up, share what is on their minds, and talk through things rationally. They should be able to make agreements and decisions that stick. If you can't control your temper, you have become the problem.

Getting angry doesn't solve the problem. It is a distraction and keeps you from finding the real solution.

SINLESS ANGER

The Bible says that we should be angry and not sin. (Ephesians 4:17) So, what is sinless anger? Anger is an emotion and a behavior. Like sadness, you don't have to cry. With anger, you don't have to say ugly words and throw things. One can feel angry and not go a little too far in expressing it. You can simply say "I'm angry." Anger, the emotion, lets us know something is wrong, that some need has gone unmet, some rule has been violated, or some expectation has been disappointed. If we are not careful, we will confuse anger 'The behavior' with anger 'The emotion.' We will attempt to use angry behavior to solve our problems. This is a very ineffective way to resolve your angry feelings. Unless you are a bully. And you know bullying is a failure.

Anger as an emotion is not inherently evil but becomes evil when it is accompanied by evil thoughts or deeds. The Ten Commandments provide the standard for us to judge right from wrong. "The fear of the LORD [is] to hate evil: pride, and arrogance, and the evil way, and the forward (sins of speech) mouth, do I hate." (Proverbs 8:13 KJV) Hatred and vengeance are certainly contrary to the law which says thou shalt not kill or do anything to harm others.

Sin is falling short of God's plan for your life. (Romans 3:23) He created us with the intention that we experience his love, peace, harmony, and joy forever. While God hurts when we hurt, he will allow evil and difficulty in our lives. And all of us will suffer to some degree in this life. He wants to get the glory for helping us through our trials. He tells us to be prepared for difficulties and challenges. (1 Peter 4:12) If we lose our temper when things go wrong, that suggests that we were not prepared for things to go wrong. It means we haven't come to a point in our maturity where we are relying on God. Anger 'The behavior' is our selfish attempt to fix what is wrong without God. It is a faithless condition. It is operating in the flesh rather than in the Spirit. (Galatians 5:19-21)

Three biblical examples of the unproductive results of impulsive anger outbursts are Cain, Moses, and the apostle Peter. Cain's problem was that he was jealous of his brother's success in gaining God's approval. In a fit of anger, he solved the problem by eliminating his brother. He no longer had any more competition. But he had to live the rest of his life under a curse for what he had done. Moses had a group of people following him who were not very intelligent. Their short-term memory was severely impaired. They were doubting the God who had just parted the Red Sea for them to escape their enemies. Moses exploded in a fit of rage at their complaints and struck the rock when God had instructed him to speak to the rock. His consequence was not being allowed in the promised land. Peter's anger caused him to forget that Jesus, the guy he was supposedly protecting, had allowed him to walk on water. He called himself protecting Jesus when he cut off the ear of the soldier who was arresting Jesus. Each of these examples provides an example of sinning when we are angry.

Sinless anger occurs when we feel anger but resist the temptation to carelessly attack others or ourselves.

Expressing anger in loving ways is something God would have you do. A soft answer turns away wrath. (Proverbs 15:1 NKJV) If you are having a difficult time managing your anger look at the resentment (underlying fear) you are holding in your heart.

RESENTMENT

Resentment is often the fuel that drives anger.

Resentment is what you hold in your heart against someone. It is unforgiven offenses that have stacked up to prove a point about how this person is or how they feel about you. It comes from a sense that others are intentionally trying to hurt you.

But most often within marriage, this conclusion is irrational. The evil that you believe was intentional is just a mistake, addiction, or a fault of your spouse. Not something you really should take personally. While it may feel like your spouse is intentionally trying to make you miserable, they are dealing with their demons. You are holding in your heart something that doesn't belong to you. You have no control over what others say or do. You have made yourself the center of attention.

Resentment is the substance of marital ire. As the couple experiences repeated injuries, resentment builds. An unsavory reputation of one another develops and causes the injured one to look for the injury to occur again. There is a fear that they will hurt you again. This is when couples begin to show contempt toward one another. This is that "you disgust me" attitude that casts a dark shadow over a couple's love. Resentment is often displayed as contempt. An example of resentment would be when one spouse feels over a long period that their spouse is not doing their part around the house. When resentment has developed, they may not recognize what their spouse actually does around the house. Whenever the topic comes up, they are combative and negative. Individuals may begin to feel taken advantage of or used. Instead of being appreciated and cherished. And they will begin to see this in almost every interaction.

Everyone must learn to respect their mate despite their faults. Resentment is built on the belief that your spouse is stupid or evil. You may have legitimate reasons to resent or disrespect your spouse, but you will never repair your marriage by continuing to keep these resentments buried in your heart. Respect is believing that you married an intelligent person although flawed and sometimes wrong. You both have different brains and will see everything somewhat differently. However, you must respect each other's intelligence. While you may not agree, it is important to show respect by listening and not arguing.

Assume that you cannot change the way the other person thinks and stop trying. Learn how to respectfully get along. Unconditional love requires forgiveness, patience, and acceptance. You must appreciate your spouse as is. If their behavior is unacceptable you will need to decide what you will do about it. Holding resentment in your heart is holding you back from moving forward. Seek to resolve the problem rather than allow the problem to fester. Face the problem rather than put up barriers to protect it.

Ryan had developed resentment toward Tiffany as he interpreted her behavior as controlling and domineering. When she asked him a simple question, he would say something sarcastic or snappy as if she had done something wrong. This was very hurtful to Tiffany as she was simply asking a question to keep the lines of communication open. This knee-jerk reaction of Ryan was pushing Tiffany further away. He had to learn to see her differently. He had to have compassion for her - thinking about her needs over his needs. He had to take responsibility for how he had come to see her and begin to see her as the loving woman he married. He had to see her as his helper, not his attacker.

DEFENSIVENESS

Defensiveness is usually the result of not feeling heard and respected. It is the result of feeling attacked or neglected. When you feel attacked the fleshly reaction is to retaliate. Back and forth, a couple goes, as one missile launch instigates another. This cycle of defensiveness is difficult to break. A couple must learn new ways of relating. They must show compassion toward each other. Defensiveness is a communication blocker. Eliminating these blockers will enhance the respect level you both feel within your marriage because you are now listening to each other.

If you are struggling with anger, resentment, and/or defensiveness make an investment in yourself and get some therapy. In therapy, you can use an unbiased third party to reduce the tension so you can gain an understanding of each other and reopen the lines of communication.

Tiffany would become defensive when Ryan would snip at her. Her defensive response was not like some who would snap back. Her response was to shut down and say nothing at all. Like an injured puppy she would hide her emotions and slip away to a quiet place to sulk. Tiffany had to learn to speak up and share when she felt offended by Ryan without becoming aggressive. She had to realize that Ryan was dealing with his guilt and his interpretation of her behavior. She learned to put the ball back into his hands when he tried to shift the blame on her. This way she could stop feeling responsible for Ryan's anger and no longer have a need to defend herself.

LOVE TANK DRAINING BEHAVIORS

It is important to understand what thoughts have contributed to the resentment and to talk it out using effective communication. Some behaviors aren't compatible with marriage and drain the love tank. Some examples of these unacceptable behaviors are not having sex, dominating and controlling your mate, extended silent treatment, complaining about your mate to others, lying and going behind your spouse's back, doing things that your spouse has specifically asked you not to do, having inappropriate relations with others outside of the marriage, not fulfilling your financial obligations, not helping around the house, yelling and putting your mate down, hitting your mate, forgetting important things, putting others before your spouse, contradicting your spouse in front of the kids, etc. These kinds of behaviors drain the love tank. If you are going to get the sizzle back, you must eliminate the contrary behaviors and attitudes. You must fill your spouse's love tank. You do this by doing the things that make them feel loved and being kind to them. If you are feeling defensive, resentment, and anger, you will be unable to be kind and loving and demonstrate the calm compassion your spouse needs to feel close to you.

EMOTION REGULATION PROBLEMS

If you are frequently upset with your spouse, you probably have an emotion regulation problem. You are having difficulty managing your emotions. Even if you don't curse and throw things you are having anger management issues.

High-conflict couples usually have emotion regulation problems. Frequently feeling anxiety, frustration, anger, and depression are signs of emotion regulation problems. Someone who frequently gets upset feels entitled to have things go how they want all the time. They constantly perceive things as going against them. They are not flexible enough to make adjustments. If this sounds like you, you need to adjust your expectations and accept that even if things are not perfect, or if bad things happen, God will make it all work out for your good in the end. See Romans 8:28.

THE FIVE T'S OF EMOTION MANAGEMENT

Ultimately you are responsible for your emotions and must take action to control them. You can't wait on someone else to help you feel better. The Five T's of Emotion Management may help you better manage your emotions.

1. Touch the part of your body where you feel upset

2. Take a few deep breaths

3. Talk positive thoughts to yourself

4. Take action to solve the problem

5. Trust God to do what you can't

TAKE RESPONSIBILITY FOR YOUR EMOTIONS

If you are going to get control of your emotions, you must take responsibility for them. Stop blaming others for how you feel and accept that your feelings are based on your thoughts and your interpretation of events. The reason why we get panicky is that we feel helpless when it comes to our emotions, and we may end up lashing out and attacking others to get rid of those bad emotions. Obviously, those attempts are irrational.

How can another person control your emotions? Take responsibility for managing your emotions. No one else can do it for you. In addition, you should allow your spouse to be responsible for their emotions. Mind your own emotions is a great policy in marriage.

In some situations, anger turns violent. Unfortunately, one or both individuals are physically wounded or even killed. Ask anyone who hurt or killed their spouse if this eased any of their negative emotions. Of course not. You must stop projecting upon others and take responsibility for your emotions. Acting out those blaming thoughts only reinforces those irrational thoughts. No one can make you feel sad, angry, hurt, rejected, abandoned, tricked, or enraged. Those emotions belong to you, and only you can resolve them. Even if your spouse sincerely apologized for what they did to you, you don't have to forgive them or feel better. They have no control over your emotions - you do. You need to examine your thoughts more closely and take responsibility for how you feel and behave. Become more selective in what you think about and practice thinking thoughts that help you feel and act the way you want and that help you reach your goals. Dealing with problems directly and not allowing negative emotions to linger is the most productive plan of action. You may need a professional to help you do this.

THE CIRCLE OF CONTROL

We often get confused about what we actually have control over and what we don't. Taking responsibility for yourself is a big deal. Not taking responsibility for others is a bigger deal. You need to be clear about what you are supposed to do and not do.

The circle of control is a great way to determine what you have control over. Draw a big circle on a blank sheet of paper. Everything on this sheet represents your life. You are concerned about everything on this sheet. But only the things that are inside the circle can you do something about. You can only control the things that are inside your circle. Things inside the circle are your hair color, what you decide to wear that day, and what route you take home.

Everything out of the circle, like your spouse, your past, and the future, you may be concerned about, but you can't control. Trying to fix, work on, and manipulate things outside the circle will only make you frustrated, angry, and upset. Not to mention how frustrated, angry and upset you will make others feel. You can use your influence, the things you say and do, to impact some things outside your circle - like others. You can influence the future by planning, preparing, and practicing, but you can't control the future. Your stress level will greatly decrease if you learn to focus on what you have the power to control or influence. If you are feeling anxiety or worry, you are operating outside your circle. The Serenity Prayer reminds us to stay in our circle.

"God grant me the serenity to accept the things I cannot change, the courage to change the things I can, and the wisdom to know the difference."

PEBBLES, ROCKS, AND BOULDERS

Another strategy for managing stress is to categorize your conflicts as pebbles, rocks, and boulders. Pebbles are unimportant, insignificant, and mundane. They are a matter of preference. They really don't matter in the great scheme of things. How you fold the towels is really a pebble. Rocks are more important and may deserve your attention and energy but certainly are not so critical that they always deserve your attention and energy. Rocks are values like time and money. The towels not getting folded may be a Rock and deserve an agreement on the matter of whether our home is going to be orderly or not. Boulders are important and critical. Boulders are deal breakers. They deserve your focus and intervention because not doing so would simply be irresponsible. The towels not getting washed is a Boulder. The towels must be washed.

We can't keep using the same dirty towels. That would be a health hazard. Spending your attention and energy on this problem is necessary and essential for your household.

Rocks and Boulders may deserve a discussion. But there is never a need for an argument. Two adults should be able to have a conversation without getting so emotional. That is the only way to resolve your differences. Bad behaviors like raising your voice, intimidating, blaming, accusing, and the like during an argument is never acceptable. A Boulder issue requires attention when a Pebble or Rock may need to be overlooked. The truth is that most of the things the couple argue about are Pebbles. The problem with individuals who have emotion management issues is that they tend to turn Pebbles and Rocks into Boulders. If you have to be right or have the last word, you are controlling the narrative. You are most likely turning everything into a Boulder. Simply to appease your pride.

In addition to understanding which category to place arguments in, couples need to be aware of their level of escalation and intensity. Your level of intensity can be seen in how upset or angry you become. A conversation having no escalation is held at a conversational level and tone. Medium escalation occurs when your concern level becomes obvious. You may frown or raise your voice. You are at maximum escalation when you are yelling, calling names, or completely shutting down. It's your choice how you categorize conflicts and it's your choice the level of escalation you take things.

A Pebble can be addressed from any level of escalation as a Boulder can be addressed from any level of escalation.

Ultimately, losing control of yourself is bad behavior and only creates more problems. Learn to recognize what's most important and how to deal with things calmly.

How many times have you had a bad argument with your spouse and couldn't later remember what you were arguing about? More than likely, it's because it was a Pebble.

Focus On the Right Thing

Learning to discern what to focus on can be very helpful in eliminating the negativity and stabilizing your mood toward each other.

Couples who have developed a *Sizzle Mindset* have learned how to stay calm and control their temper. They are careful to speak kindly to one another when angry and upset. They know how to make happiness happen. They know how important it is to be loving toward your spouse regardless of your differences. If you focus too much on being right or getting your partner to do right, you end up hurting your spouse. Even if they hurt you, it's not worth hurting them back. Doing so you ultimately hurt yourself. Learn to make happiness happen.

Ryan began to realize that his anger was not producing a loving response toward Tiffany. He had to make some adjustments in how he saw her aggression so he could calm down and feel more content and peaceful toward her.

Tiffany's anxiety was out of control. She had to realize that the world was not about to end so she could calm down. She began to shift how Ryan felt about her outside her circle. She had to allow him to think and behave as he saw fit. She had to love him the way he was and pray for God to change him. This effectively reduced her anxiety and allowed her to stay present even when Ryan was going off on a tangent. As both made these changes, they restored peace in their relationship. They learned how important managing their own emotions and being calm was to maintain the sizzle in their marriage.

REFLECTION

On a scale of 1 to 10, 10 being the highest, how calm are you in your marital relationship?

On a scale of 1 to 10, 10 being the highest, how calm is your partner in your relationship?

CHAPTER SEVEN
Community

Be Talkative, Be Sexy & Be Healthy

Community is a unified body of individuals who share something in common. Whether it's a neighborhood, a swimming club, a social media group, a workplace, or an entire city, a group of people who share some affiliation form a community. The people who live together under one roof are a community. This community is often referred to as family.

Marriage is a social institution. A community of two. If you are having difficulties in your marriage, it is because you are having social problems. You are having difficulties getting along. You are having challenges making agreements. People have difficulties getting along because they don't share the same values and expectations, or they are conflicting over their values and expectations. They have difficulty listening to each other, being flexible, and finding creative ways to solve their problems. Their conflicts are frequent misunderstandings, miscommunication, or misapprehension. Somewhere along the way, the message that was intended was not received. When there is confusion among any size group of people community breaks down. As community breaks down the purpose of the community gets fuzzy. When the reason for affiliation is unclear the community will eventually fizzle out and disappear.

When the two who have come together to form a household no longer feel the benefits of companionship, shared values, and goals, they begin to consider ending the relationship. If you and your spouse are having social challenges, you are not meeting each other's social needs. This is because you aren't listening to each other. Your individual agendas supersede your community agenda. If you want a healthy marriage, you must ensure that each other's needs are being met. This can only be accomplished when you listen to each other and sincerely care.

Community is built by recreating and spending time together as a family. It is built upon the agreements you have made when establishing your relationship. When you default on those agreements you place your relationship in jeopardy. You end up destroying your community with absence, isolation, meanness, disrespect and controlling behavior. We all need to feel like we belong. Like we are a part of something bigger than ourselves. We all need comradery, celebration, encouragement, and accountability. We need acceptance, affirmation, and affection. We can't provide for our own social needs. We can only act like they don't exist. But they do and when this need for belonging and being taken care of is not met, we often act out in anger, and resentment, and find ourselves returning evil for evil.

A failed marriage is an indication that one or both partners lack the social skills necessary to enjoy a peaceful and harmonious union. So many divorce and remarry someone else in hopes of finding a suitable partner. Couples usually divorce blaming the other for their failed marriage.

However, the divorce rates for second and third marriages are higher than for first marriages. This is evidence that what is frequently missing in unhappy marriages is not the right partner, it's the qualities needed to enjoy a happy marriage.

These qualities include effective communication, problem-solving, emotion management, forgiveness, faith, maturity, wisdom, understanding, discernment, patience, courage, boldness, love, discipline, self-control, etc.

These qualities can be developed when we bury our pride and allow God to work on us. He will use various means to root out our selfishness and develop good character in us. Often it is in the fire of trouble and difficulties where God does his greatest work in us.

At our very core, we are only interested in ourselves. This selfish, self-centered perspective is anti-social. You can't only serve yourself and enjoy being a part of a healthy community. In many instances, in order to enjoy relationships with others, we must subdue our selfish interests. Or else, you will be alone.

To build a *Sizzling Hot Marriage* couples must have confidence in each other's unconditional love and commitment, establish that meeting their spouses' needs is the top priority, and establish that we are "one" to the rest of the world. Start doing things together again. Have fun! Walk together in harmony. Smile again. Give each other compliments. This is how you re-establish community. Stop focusing on "me" and start focusing again on "we".

BE TALKATIVE

Sexual desire is the essential reason why we decide to get married. You fall in love with someone you find sexually attractive. Sexual attraction includes much more than physical appeal. It includes your perception of what this companionship and partnership will mean for your life.

Some relationships start off with sex. This is dangerous because sex should be a continuation of the conversation.

Couples who start out sexually often don't have the foundation they need to sustain a long-term relationship.

Conversation is the fuel of community. The ability to talk about anything anytime is what a healthy companionship looks like. Couples who can talk through the ups and downs of life have a great chance of making it. When talking stops, couples are in trouble of losing a sense of their purpose.

Men are usually stimulated by what they see. Women are the actual act of sex doesn't usually take very long. If that is all a man has to offer a woman, she will be woefully unfulfilled. Most women need robust conversations to feel their companionship needs are being met. But don't be mistaken, men need this as well. It's just that men are often not socialized to talk about what is on their minds. They are taught that being strong is being independent and not asking for help. God didn't intend for any of us to be an isolated island unto ourselves. Unfortunately, many men and women have not learned to open up and share what is on their mind. They don't trust anyone and keep things balled up inside. You will not be able to sustain a relationship this way. If you desire to enjoy a healthy community, you must be able to disclose your thoughts and feelings in a way that is effectively received.

Women are usually stimulated by what they feel emotionally. For women, these emotional feelings are usually stirred by enjoyable conversations that signify companionship, security, and love. Long conversations and walks in the park make women feel like they have someone to talk to and share their lives with. Men are usually so focused on catching the next meal they may feel like a casual conversation is a waste of time. It is important for men and women to find a common ground for the meeting of the minds. Couples who fail to spend at least five hours of undivided attention weekly are going to find it difficult to find their sexual groove. If sex is intermittent, the couple is not giving their marriage enough undivided attention - focus time to talk, resolve problems, and build their intimate connection.

Disagreement is the central reason couples generate bad vibes between them. Problems pop up and choices are made individually rather than as a couple. Unable to communicate effectively the problem remains unresolved and the relationship begins to unravel. Unresolved problems are like a sink clogged with hair and other debris. You know there is a problem when the water starts to drain slower than usual. If there is no intervention, the drain will eventually become completely clogged.

This is the beautiful thing about counseling that makes me enjoy the service that I provide. The counselor is skilled to help you unclog that communication drain. The therapist will help you navigate the communication blockage that the two of you have developed. Therapy is about listening to your heart and helping your partner hear too. Whether you are blessed to have a counselor or not, talking through your problems is a must if you are going to have a *Sizzling Hot Marriage.*

Solve Your Solvable Problems

The secret to keeping the passion alive in your marriage is learning how to talk about sensitive issues. A *Sizzle Mindset* makes love a priority when talking to one another.

Many couples have some very serious issues to work through. To get the sizzle back in your marriage you need to resolve those serious problems that have been plaguing your marriage.

Have in-laws been a problem? They live next door and keep coming over without asking. This has created severe conflict between the two of you because your spouse doesn't have a problem with it. You have complained and argued, to no avail. What the two of you need is to become better communicators. This issue shouldn't become an argument.

You should be able to sit down and have an adult discussion about the problem in a conversational tone. You should remain respectful of each other's perspectives and seek to find an agreeable solution. Neither one of you should think that you should have your way all the time. You should be open to compromise and negotiation. If the two of you can't come up with an agreeable solution, you should be open to seeking a professional adviser who can help you develop an agreeable approach to the problem. Get whatever help you need to talk through the issues and work toward solutions.

If you open the lines of communication, you will be able to find an agreeable solution. Maybe you'd come to agree to have a conversation with your parents about the problem, setting up some boundaries and rules you need them to respect. Maybe you decided to say something like "Hey mom and dad, we need our privacy. Can you plan to come over on Friday nights instead of at any time?" "And if you would like to come over any other time, would you please call to find out if it's OK with us?"

Find a way to identify those long-standing problems and talk until you find a solution. That may also mean going to get some professional help to talk about the problem. Don't give up. Get the issue fixed.

Are you struggling with a sexual issue? Men often complain about not having enough sex. Women often complain about the lack of affection, romance, and foreplay. Becoming effective communicators would entail scheduling a time to talk, using the tile method to take turns talking, and discussing various solutions to solve the problem. If you are able to open the lines of communication, maybe you'd decide to schedule your sexual encounters and take turns planning some romance into your sex dates. You decide to play some of your favorite jams to set the mood and anticipation. Do you agree on lingerie or not and whether you would give each other a scented oil massage? You may end up discussing the details of the sexual moment. Like determining you need more time before penetration and discovering methods to delay ejaculation. You may consider adding some lubricant or a vibrator to your sexual routine. You may consider exploring some different positions or places to have sex. Couples have discovered in their experimentation that their bed was not firm enough to do the job.

Taking the time to talk through sexual issues brings about a solution and is helpful in getting the sizzle back in your marriage. When you are able to talk about anything anytime, you open the door to deep intimacy and connection.

If you want to get the sizzle back into your marriage you need to be proactive, assertive, and diligent about discussing things. It's going to require some effort and energy on both of your parts to have intentional discussions with the aim to solve problems.

Love is a beautiful thing, but you must take care of it. Avoiding talking about the problems is only going to make matters worse. Much like a plant that needs to be watered, fertilized, weeded, and given plenty of sunshine to grow, your marriage needs to be tended to grow.

Not every problem is solvable. Remember the Pebbles, Rocks, and Boulders illustration? Happy couples learn to distinguish between what problems must be solved and those that don't. They recognize that many Pebbles and Rocks may best be left up to God to resolve.

Couples who take time to talk are much happier and more satisfied in their marriage. Infidelity issues are one of the toughest conversations to have with your spouse. Here are some tips on having that conversation.

TALKING THROUGH AN AFFAIR

Effective communication is being able to tell your spouse what you heard them say in a way that makes them feel like you fully comprehended and valued what they said. You may not agree but that is OK if you truly listened. It is very important to understand one's motives for their behavior. Take an affair as an example. The betrayed spouse may take no responsibility for the affair but upon closer inspection, you might find the couple had been struggling for quite some time with communication problems.

I've heard many excuses for affairs over the years: One of the most frequent excuses was looking to find solace and a listening ear. Another might be an attempt to get one's physical needs met that were not being met in the marriage. Others simply state that it was an opportunity they didn't have the discipline to say no to. While one would like to blame their spouse for having an affair, one must take full responsibility for their behavior.

The marital relationship may have nothing to do with the affair. But the affair has a tremendous impact on the marriage. Whether the marriage had problems before the affair it will have problems afterwards. Effective communication can close those gaps and affair-proof the marriage. Professional counseling can facilitate this conversation.

After an affair, or anything like an affair, the underlying dependency or unresolved emotional issue must be worked on while you are rebuilding your relationship. In this case, however, you will more than likely need a professional who is positioned to help you work on your marriage and your underlying issues concurrently. Couples should seek professional help after an affair whether they decide to stay together or part ways. Counseling will help you balance focusing on the spouse who had the affair and focusing on your marriage.

An affair is an opportunity to address the issues in your marriage and the individual issues that are contributing to your relationship dynamics. Not all therapists and counselors are able or equipped to do this as many advisers see marriage as disposable and will not work skillfully to preserve your union. No matter where you live you can find a therapist who can help you work through the underlying issues that may be handicapping your marriage. Like myself many provide telephone and video consulting. Even if you live in a remote area there is no excuse for not getting the help you need.

Both of you should feel comfortable with your therapist right away. I believe this is probably the most important way to see if a therapist will be good for you. You should also see some positive results from your encounters with your therapist soon. However, beware of the "I don't like the therapist" smoke screen. Some spouses will never like any therapist because they know they are the problem, and they are not ready to acknowledge and be held accountable to make changes. In my opinion, if that is the case, you need to ask them if they want to stay married to you. Let them know that the issues at hand are very important to you and must be resolved if you are to stay married. Don't allow your spouse to stonewall you unless you are willing to lower the importance of your issue with your spouse.

Divorce is a solution to marital problems. But it should only be the last resort. After many years of dealing with someone who constantly disregards your agreements, divorce seems to be the only option. I think you should seriously consider divorce when your partner continues to blame you for their bad behaviors and refuses to take personal responsibility. If they dismiss you and say go ahead and divorce them, you must seriously consider divorce. Many times, they are still wrapped up emotionally in the person they were cheating with. Having a professional walk, you through this process can be very helpful.

If your spouse continues to blame you for their bad behaviors, don't count on them to change. A spouse who refuses to take personal responsibility for their indiscretions must be held accountable. You must establish clear boundaries with people who are verbally, emotionally, physically, or sexually abusive. You must take a stand against continued abuse. If they refuse to admit they are hurting you, they will continue to hurt you. Why stay in a relationship with someone who continues to blame you for their bad behavior. Until you hold them accountable, they will not change. The only hope for change for these individuals is therapy. If they don't submit to therapy, they don't believe they have a problem. They are continuing to blame others for their bad behaviors. Don't continue to deal with a spouse who continues to hurl insults when you remind them of their infidelity. If they don't submit to therapy, they are not serious about taking personal responsibility for their bad behaviors. If they are not serious about taking personal responsibility, a year from now you will be in the same situation.

Here are a couple of warnings. Be careful not to give up the process too soon. Don't quit one counselor before you find another. If you want things to change, it is not the therapist who has to do the work. You should do the work.

Don't get mad at the therapist when the therapist calls you out. You must remember that it's your mindset that is causing you problems in your marriage. The therapist offers a different perspective that will feel strange and wrong. Be careful to stay open to these new perspectives as they offer you the mindset shift you need to transform your marriage. If you feel offended by the therapist talk it out. The therapist is a professional but is also human. Everyone has a right to their own opinion.

After a few therapy sessions, you may begin to feel better. Don't make the mistake many couples make and stop the process before the new mindset has had the opportunity to solidify. Old habits die hard. It takes nearly two months to establish a new habit. Don't assume a few sessions is all you need. Hang in there until you have completed the course. You will need to talk through your affair many times before the freshness of the hurt stales and credibility rebuilds. You will need to be able to talk with each other about the affair without it becoming a blow up. To get to this point, it takes time.

ELIMINATE CRITICISM

Are you a cup-half-full or half-empty kind of person? You drain the love tank by criticizing your mate; they want to feel like you like them. Can't you find something good in them to focus on? Paul reminds us that kindness and gentleness need to be our standard in our relationships with others. (Galatians 5:22) How you say what is on your mind is just as important as what you say. You can say things in a negative critical way or a positive boosting way.

"Let no corrupt communication proceed out of your mouth, but that which is good to the use of edifying, that it may minister grace unto the hearers. And grieve not the Holy Spirit

99

of God, whereby ye are sealed unto the day of redemption. Let all bitterness, and wrath, and anger, and clamor, and evil speaking, be put away from you, with all malice: And be ye kind one to another, tenderhearted, forgiving one another, even as God for Christ's sake hath forgiven you." (Ephesians 4:29-32 KJV)

This text is the epitome, the perfect example of how to *Return to Love*. Most couples who have fallen out of love have stopped being kind and tender toward each other. They have become judgmental or stale toward each other. If you have formulated a negative view of your spouse it may be very difficult for your spouse to dig their way out of that hole. Negative criticism and complaining will not help your marriage. It may be true that sometimes the criticism is well deserved. However, criticism arises out of a judgmental controlling spirit and is not usually well received. It is measuring others by ourselves which Paul tells us is not wise. (1 Corinthians 10:12) Criticism is fear-based as it assumes something bad is going to happen.

The problem is that this negative spirit frequently erupts during disagreements. An emotional landslide occurs when both parties become emotionally unbalanced. Tempers flare (whether expressed or not) and hatred, rather than love is projected upon the other. Many couples are high-conflict couples. Their fight or flight syndrome gets triggered rather frequently and they find themselves embroiled in a fight maybe even daily. Many times, one spouse is pursuing while the other is running, both are running, or both are fighting.

Regardless, the mood is elevated, and hatred is being communicated rather than love.

Couples with a *Sizzle Mindset* avoid this negativity and are careful to remain kind and tenderhearted toward each other. If they have something critical to say they speak it in love. (Ephesians 4:15) Not only do they avoid negativity but they are engaged in a conversation that flows from day to day.

They talk to each other about everything. If you are going to keep passion alive in your marriage, the lines of communication must remain open.

Tiffany realized that the way she talked to Ryan was wrong. She spoke to him like he was her child. She decided to be more respectful in her tone and facial expression when she shared her opinion about things. This had a tremendously positive impact on Ryan as it made it easier for him to receive her criticism and listen to what she had to say. They were now able to talk things out instead of avoiding one another.

This made them feel so much closer to one another. Their ability to talk more has led to greater levels of passion in their marriage.

BE SEXY

Sex is a continuation of the conversation. Men are usually stimulated by what they see. Women are usually stimulated by what they feel emotionally. For women, these emotional feelings are usually stirred by enjoyable conversations that signify companionship, security, and love. Couples who fail to spend at least five hours of undivided attention weekly are going to find it difficult to find their sexual groove. If sex is intermittent the couple is not giving their marriage enough undivided attention - focus time to talk, resolve problems, and build their intimate connection.

A big part of bringing happiness to your spouse is satisfying them sexually. Wasn't it that sex appeal that attracted you to one another in the first place? Being sexy simply means being appealing and attracted to one another. It seems that after the initial excitement of marriage wears off many have amnesia and forget to do the things that initially appealed to their spouse. You must work to stay attractive to your spouse. Many don't like the idea that marriage is work because it makes it sound like something they don't want to do. Maybe a better word is positive energy. Marriage requires positive energy. It takes energy to fight your spouse. It also takes energy to fulfill the requests of your spouse. During courtship, most couples are putting a lot of positive energy into the relationship. After marriage and the honeymoon period many slip into their lazy mode where they are giving very little positive energy to their spouse. This is called bait and switch in the retail world. It takes energy to keep a fire burning. You should keep throwing logs on the fire if you plan to keep the fire burning.

What are you doing to keep the fires of love burning in your marriage? Couples who develop a *Sizzle Mindset* understand how important it is to be sexy with one another. Having sex is an opportunity to celebrate the relationship and renew the love.

If you have lost your sizzle the good news is that you can get it back. Fill your spouse's empty love tank and you can feel the fire again. The love tank is a great analogy useful for communicating where you are in your relationship at any given point. You fill their love tank by loving them in their language. Gary Chapman, in his book The Five Love Languages, teaches us that everyone has a primary and secondary love language. He explains that we tend to love others in our language. Some people's love language is physical touch. When they are touched, they feel loved. Another person may prefer words of affirmation–tell me how beautiful I am, tell me how much you appreciate me. Someone else's love language may be gifts–buy me something or write me a card. Another person's love language may be acts of service– do something nice for me. Don't just sit there watching football all day, get up and wash the dishes, cut the lawn, take my car to the car wash, think about it and surprise me with something that I would have never thought you would do. Or do something without me asking you to do it.

Someone else's love language might be quality time–let's go for a walk, let's sit around and talk, let's take some time out together, let's take a ride to the country together. If you don't love your spouse in their language, they may not feel loved. Figure out whether your spouse's love language is gifts, acts of service, quality time, physical touch, or words of affirmation. You could be knocking yourself out buying stuff for them and miss the mark because their language is words of affirmation. You may be loving them in your language but all they need you to do is say "I love you"

When your love tank is full you feel like loving. But when your love tank is empty, you don't. You want to make sure that your spouse's love tank is full, and that the only person who can fill that love tank is you. You don't want anybody else filling your spouse's love tank, do you? That is why it's so important for your partner to share with you what's on their mind; what they feel would be helpful to you. Why would you argue with your customer? If you are there to serve your spouse, then you will listen to them when they share what they need from you.

WHAT TO DO WHEN THAT IN-LOVE FEELING IS GONE

When couples go unsatisfied in their marriage over an extended period, they often come to a point where they say that the emotional feelings for one another are simply gone. They don't feel connected emotionally anymore, and they don't feel any romantic feelings toward the other person. They get tired of all the conflict and the struggle to love and to be loved. I frequently hear "it shouldn't be this hard". If this negativity persists, without intervention it is highly unlikely conditions will occur to stimulate the love between you. You may come to a point where you feel drained completely and have no feelings at all. Lots of couples conclude that they just need to separate or divorce and end their marriage at that point. Divorce shouldn't be your first go to when you reach this state. A few relationship tweaks will usually suffice to reverse those lost love feelings.

The truth is that feelings come and go. Our feelings toward one another are based on our experience with each other and what's going on in our lives. If you are critical, negative, and/ or controlling with your spouse, over time you will drain their love tank and they will no longer feel like loving you. Those warm fuzzy feelings will not be there, and they will want to avoid you. But if you become a more positive loving person, you will fill their love tank and they will begin feeling those love feelings again. Like yesterday's meal, what was done or not done yesterday is a thing of the past. I need to feel loved today.

Believe it or not you can feel those love feelings again. Don't despair and don't get discouraged if you're not feeling the same way you used to feel for one another. Just *Return to Love* by eliminating the negativity and plugging up the holes in the love tank. A mother doesn't enjoy the pain of childbirth, but it's soon forgotten when the child arrives. You will soon forget all the negativity you once felt when you start loving each other again.

To get the sizzle back in your marriage you need to become a better lover. You need to discipline yourself to *Return to Love* when your spouse disappoints you. I have heard many men excuse their behavior by saying "I'm not good at that romantic stuff." That is like the mechanic saying to their customer "I'm not good at fixing cars." So, what will that customer do? That's right–go to another shop. If you don't want your wife (husband) going to another shop, you better figure out how to be a better lover. Jim Rohn says, 'What is easy to do is easy not to do." It is easy to say, "I love you". It is easy to set down every day to talk eye-to-eye with your spouse. It is easy to buy a card for your spouse. It is easy to wash the dishes every day. It is easy to give your spouse a long passionate hug and kiss every day. But what is easy to do is easy not to do.

When you look at what is recorded about Jesus in the New Testament, you see Him constantly concerned about people's needs. He healed the sick and reunited deceased children with their parents. He fed people when they were hungry and helped the crippled walk again. He provided more wine at a wedding when all the wine had run out. He died for sinners so they wouldn't have to die for themselves. Jesus was and is always doing for others. The Bible says He did for others and didn't even have a place to lay His head. (Matthew 8:20)

What about you? Have you been more worried about what your spouse is or isn't doing for you? What are you doing for your spouse? What need of your spouse are you not meeting? Love is acting to meet those needs. Remember the Bible says you reap what you sow. (Galatians 6:7) Sow into your spouse and you will reap a harvest. Engage in loving behaviors to build a loving relationship. Even if your spouse is unloving toward you, you don't have to be unloving toward them. You can return love for evil and not evil for evil.

Decide that you're going to be a more loving spouse and that you're going to be a more forgiving spouse. Take time to figure out your partner's love language and come up with ideas of how you can love them in their language. There are hundreds of ways to love your spouse. Come up with thirty things that you can do to love your spouse. Take the next thirty days to do one of them each day. Buy them a bouquet of flowers, write I love you with soap on the mirror, detail their car, etc. I guarantee you that they'll be much sweeter for it. In fact, you will be much happier. If you want to be happy you must make others happy and build a little heaven down here.

By doing these things you will make yourself more appealing to your spouse. This is making love.

Couples who make making love a priority have more fulfilling marriages. Your sexual relationship must be in the context of a loving relationship where you both put forth the energy to love (the verb) one another. A *Sizzle Mindset* remembers to love their spouse in their language every day. Couples that get this right end up having more frequent and mutually satisfying sexual encounters each week. Just like they wouldn't deprive one another of food they are careful to not deny one another sexually. It is easy to have sex with someone you feel loves and cares for you. Keeping one another's love tank full is the secret to keeping passion alive in your marriage.

Ryan decided that he needed to curb his appetite for sports and pay more attention to his wife. He is careful to go to bed at the same time as Tiffany. He has also started making sure they have their couple worship time each day. Tiffany feels so much more secure in their marriage now that Ryan is focused on loving her in her language. As a result, she is much less controlling and actually gives him space to make some decisions without her criticism. A *Sizzle Mindset* has really changed things in their household. They feel so much more attracted to one another. Their sexual experience now reflects the deeper intimacy they have achieved since developing a *Sizzle Mindset*.

BE HEALTHY

They say that health is something money can't buy. If that is so, why do people with means tend to live longer healthier lives? Some communities are healthier than others. An important consideration in your community of two is identifying ways to stay healthy. As a couple, you should invest time and finances in your health. To enjoy a long, mutually satisfying sex life, couples must remain healthy physically, emotionally, socially, and financially. To enjoy a happy marriage, both of you must take an active role in keeping your marriage healthy so you can ensure a long and fulfilling marriage. Remember to remember each other's needs, practice patience and understanding towards your partner, and be willing to compromise. This will help create an environment where both partners feel heard and respected.

Staying healthy should remain a priority for couples. You should consider together how you can be healthier as a couple. What do you both need to be healthier physically, emotionally, socially, and financially? Take time to write out your goals in each of these areas. Here are some things you may want to consider.

Discussing health issues is often very difficult for couples. If you can open the lines of communication, you may discover how you can work together to lose weight. Focusing on getting in shape may also be something you can do together. A discussion about this may produce something very positive in your marriage. Maybe you need to discuss finances. How can we work together to build wealth?

Maybe there appears to be a growing dependency on mood altering substances or gambling. You should talk about it and reach a consensus about what you can do together to be healthier. No matter how serious the situation–the only way to move forward is to have effective communication about it.

When it comes to your physical health, you want to consider your activity level. Too many couples find themselves exhausted from a day of work relaxing in front of the TV. Watching TV together is not a good way to be physically healthy. Nor does it contribute to your undivided attention time you so desperately need to grow your marriage. It is a distraction. I encourage couples to take a three-week fast from TV focusing rather on spending time together and finding some new and old things to do together.

Couples sign up to be together. But without being intentional, they find themselves rarely spending time together. Is that what has happened to you?

Staying active by doing things together like walking, gardening, and cooking fulfills many objectives. You are spending time together, having conversations, and burning calories. Couples should agree on a healthy meal plan, an equitably shared chore list to keep the home in order, and house rules for reduced stress at home. This is how you build community in your home.

We all have some unhealthy habits that, over the long term, will have a deleterious effect on our health as we get older. Some examples might be eating too late at night, drinking too many sugary drinks, eating too much red meat, etc. Maybe you could schedule to go to the gym together two or three times a week. Make a pack with each other to find healthy replacements for those unhealthy habits. As life partners, it is important to join forces and work together to develop a healthy lifestyle to contribute to a long healthy life together.

What does it mean to be emotionally healthy?

Emotionally healthy individuals have learned how to deal effectively with their feelings. They can regulate their emotions, set boundaries, and healthily manage stress. They are also able to form healthy relationships and maintain self-esteem. Emotional health is an important component of marriage, and couples should be committed to caring for each other's emotional needs. Consider what can be done to improve your emotional health. Maybe there are some things you can do together that are relaxing and stress relieving like taking walks around the neighborhood, going on impulsive last-minute weekend trips, spending a random night in the hotel, having get-togethers with friends, visiting with family, cleaning the garage together, volunteering together, etc. Take a moment to create a bucket list of things to do to make new memories together.

An emotionally healthy marriage looks like two individuals who are deeply connected and have a mutual understanding, respect, and trust for one another. They are able to manage their own emotions while also being attuned to their partner's emotional needs. They are able to communicate effectively and openly about their feelings, provide support, and be respectful of each other. If you have difficulty achieving this, consider attending a marital communication class or marriage retreat. Schedule a few counseling sessions to work on your communication skills and improve your ability to talk through those tough topics.

By improving communication, couples can create a marriage that is strong and healthy. Establishing rules for communication, taking care of one another's emotional needs, and understanding marriage's complexities can help couples create a marriage that will last.

Are you socially healthy? Social health involves enjoying fulfilling relationships with family and friends. Couples need to have couple friends. It may take a little work for couples who don't have satisfying relationships with nearby family members and friends to develop those relationships. Some great places to find friends are work, church, clubs, volunteering, neighbors, school, marriage events, community events, parties, etc.

Enjoying each other's company is the most important social health concern to check off your list. Being able to talk about anything at any time is a crucial must-have for every marriage. Identify topics you find easy to talk about. Come up with conversation starter questions. Work on going deeper in your conversation and avoiding surface-level talk. Share your thoughts and feelings about each other's thoughts and feelings. When you become an effective communicator, you'll be able to do this.

What are your financial goals? There is always room to improve finances. Where do you need to grow in this area? Maybe you should consider having weekly financial meetings where you discuss the needs and whether you are on track to your goals. Getting on the same financial page will contribute greatly to your becoming a *Sizzling Hot Marriage*. Money represents power. Couples need to share power in their relationship. Too many couples allow money to come between them. Money is very important. But money is just a tool. Your relationship is so much more important. Everybody has financial problems from time to time. Some have long-term financial problems. Address these problems. Make plans to improve your financial situation. Talk to a financial advisor. Do what you need to do but make sure you don't allow finances to come between you.

Here's a list of health-producing practices for you to make sure you are doing.

-Communicate openly and honestly

-Listen to each other with empathy

-Seek to understand one another's perspective

-Resolve issues quickly and respectfully

-Make time for each other

-Practice patience and understanding

-Remain committed to the marriage

In summary, marriage requires effort from both partners to be healthy and strong. Couples need to work together to build a healthy lifestyle communicating openly and respectfully about their feelings, taking care of each other's emotional needs, and staying active. By practicing these principles, you can ensure a healthy marriage that will bring joy, peace, and happiness into your life. Taking an active role in nurturing your marriage is key to keeping it strong and thriving. A strong marriage not only brings stability and financial security but also leads to better parenting skills.

Ultimately marriage is an important part of life and should be taken seriously. By taking the time to work on your marriage issues, you can create a strong community that will lead to a long, satisfying, healthy union.

REFLECTION

On a scale of 1 to 10, 10 being the highest, how much community do you feel in your marriage?

On a scale of 1 to 10, 10 being the highest, how much community do you think your partner feels in your marriage?

CHAPTER EIGHT

Consistency

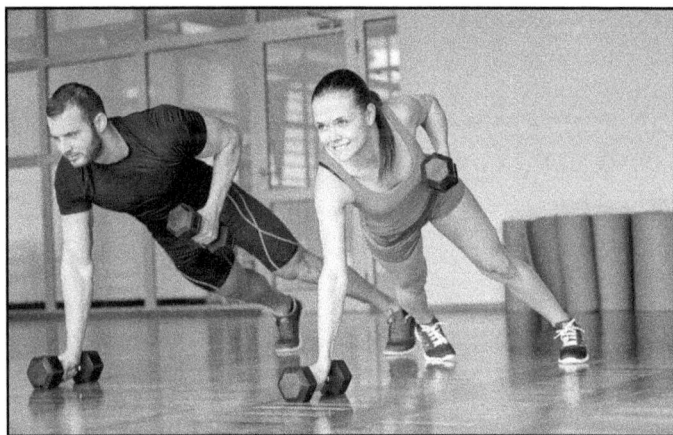

Be Mindful & Be God-centered

Consistency is the fifth pillar couples must build if they expect to have a *Sizzling Hot Marriage*. Consistency is a routine that you repeat. It is doing the same thing over and over again every day. While consistency is the secret to success in any venture we pursue, consistency can be very difficult to achieve.

As a very competitive athlete, I know it takes consistency to win the game. You have to hit that ball the same way every time if you plan to beat out the competition. The winner is the one who hits it the same way more often. Couples who are Consistent in being Credible with each other, careful to offer daily Confirmation of their love, gracious about showing Compassion, and serious about maintaining a harmonious Community are happier. They consistently fulfill their agreements.

Are you consistent in your marriage?

Simone Biles is a stellar example of consistency. During her time, she showed the world how to hit it the same way every time. If you plan to be successful in your marriage you must be consistent in confirming your love for your spouse and making your spouse your priority. You must consistently be credible - doing what you say you will do and honestly revealing your thoughts and feelings. You must remain forgiving and considerate when your spouse messes up, and make sure you preserve your identity as a couple by walking together in harmony.

Consistency comes with TIME. Winning comes from hours of practice. Like a baby learning to walk, developing consistency means you will fail. But if you keep trying, you will master loving your spouse how they need to be loved.

It can be very difficult to be consistent. Change is difficult.

We are set in our ways, and even though we know we need to do better, we find ourselves falling back into old ways. I remember my mother getting on my case about taking out the trash when it was full. I understood it was my responsibility, but I just couldn't seem to be consistent without her reminders.

It can be very annoying to have a spouse who can't seem to do what they promised. No one is perfect. However, if you say you will do something, you need to do it. Otherwise, you compromise your Credibility, Confirmation, Compassion, Community, and Consistency. If you are having problems fulfilling your commitments, you should do research to figure out why. I've discovered the reason why many spouses fail to be consistent is that they have a condition called Attention-Deficit Hyperactivity Disorder. These individuals have difficulty staying focused on tasks. There is nothing wrong with their brain; they just think differently than most people. If you or your spouse has this condition, you likely have difficulty remembering to do what you said you would do and following through when starting things. You need to seek professional help to get a proper diagnosis and treatment. You must develop a way to remind yourself and stay focused on your responsibilities.

I've counseled many women who complained about their husband's lack of affection. If you are one of those guys, don't keep making excuses. Put reminders in your phone to give a hug, touch her on the waist, or kiss her. I believe in the adage, "Do unto others what you will have them do unto you." Whatever your spouse requests, you should say yes as far as possible. Give them what they want, and they should give you what you want. That way, you can keep the lines of communication open and stay in agreement.

Just yesterday, I asked my wife to fetch a blanket for me while I was reclining on the couch. Yet a couple of hours later, she asked me to fetch a charger for her phone. She said yes, and I said yes. It works when you work it.

There are many reasons why people get married. But the one big expectation most have is companionship. Most people are looking to enjoy a lifelong friendship with their spouse. Unfortunately, conflict on how to live life leaves many couples' companionship far from fulfilling. Agreeing on how to live life together is what this book is all about. This is the work that couples must do. Once you come to an agreement, you can become consistent in doing what works for you as a couple.

Couples who are having difficulty getting in sync have not been able to agree on how they are going to live their lives. The result is a hit-and-miss inconsistent love-hate marriage. The sooner you can work to get on the same page, the sooner you can enjoy a *Sizzling Hot Marriage*.

Ryan and Tiffany decided they were not enjoying their companionship. They felt like their home was a boxing ring, with both retreating to their corners after sparring with each other. Going to therapy helped them to listen to and understand each other. Now they could have productive conversations that led to agreements they could stick to. An example was agreeing to go to bed around the same time together. They could come to this agreement only because they learned how to hear each other out and compromise.

Too many couples make agreements they don't really mean. They are just saying OK to end the conversation.

There is no way you can be consistent if you don't understand your partner.

Do you make promises you don't intend to keep?

Couples must be able to hold each other accountable in an agreed-upon manner. Whether the agreement is a keyword or phrase that neither finds offensive or a text message reminder, couples must support each other on this journey of life together. Nobody has it all together. We need each other's support. It is so easy to apologize for your bad behavior, start to do better, and then eventually fall back into your old habits. It takes about two months to establish a new habit. Consistency requires new habits built on understanding. Not capitulation - just agreeing to agree and later not following through. It is very important for couples to establish ways to hold each other accountable thus helping each be our best selves.

You must stay in an accountability cycle long enough to experience second-order change - true transformation. When transformation comes, so does consistency. Transformation means you now see things differently. When you see things differently, your motivation changes. The reason why it is so hard to stick to that diet plan or that exercise schedule is that you haven't changed your mind. You intellectually see value in doing things differently, however, you haven't yet made an emotional connection to the need for change. Once you experience the pain of what you don't want in your life or the joy of having what you want in life, there is very little motivation to do anything differently. You will go back to doing it the way you have always done it and staying in your comfort zone.

We are wired for comfort. It takes embracing discomfort for change to occur. You find yourself returning to what you have practiced and observed the most. Building this foundational pillar of consistency often requires deep personal work to deal with and reverse those limiting beliefs that keep you trapped in unproductive patterns. Just because your father or mother did it doesn't mean you have to do it.

You can choose a different path.

Being consistent is essential if you want to enjoy a *Sizzling Hot Marriage*. To build consistency in your marriage, you must learn how to be mindful and God-centered.

BE MINDFUL

Mindfulness is the practice of being aware of the many facets of life. It is maintaining a moment-by-moment awareness of our thoughts, feelings, bodily sensations, and surrounding environment, through a gentle, nurturing lens. Your ability to be aware of yourself, your spouse, and your surroundings are impaired by unresolved emotions and unmet needs. It is difficult to be mindful of your spouse's needs when you have unmet needs of your own. When you are overwhelmed by your own needs, you will be unable to be aware of your spouse's needs. To become a *Sizzling Hot Marriage*, you must shift your mindset to become more aware of yourself and your spouse.

Think about the last time you received a speeding ticket or had an accident. Do you remember how difficult it was to focus after that? I hit a curb the other day and wasn't the same for the next 24 hours. I kept rehearsing in my mind the incident and couldn't believe what I had done. I couldn't focus on much anything else. It's the same when you have unresolved issues swirling around your mind; you will not be able to fully focus on your spouse unless they are resolved.

To get the sizzle back in your marriage and keep it sizzling, you must stay mindful of your sizzle status. Keep your mind on it! This mindset involves staying conscious of the condition of your relationship. This requires continuously checking in to see how things are going and determining what improvements can be achieved. It is being aware of the growth areas and strengths in your relationship. Being mindful is being growth minded. Staying open to personal and relationship improvement keeps the flame burning.

Throughout the week, keep checking in with your spouse to see how things are going every day. Ask them how full their love tank is. Inevitably, you will get off track in your marriage.

Everybody does from time to time. Maybe a holiday season threw your weekly date night routine off track. Checking in will help you ensure months don't go by before you recognize what has happened.

Sizzling Hot Marriages don't happen by accident. They are intentional. We are prone to make mistakes and get distracted. There must always be an intentional effort to *Return to Love* in your marriage. You may find in your check-in that you have drifted apart. Checking in will encourage you to keep doing things for your marriage. You may realize you must take a vacation or go on a marriage retreat. You may want to do a marriage Bible study at church. Checking in should also include an individual check-up to see how you are spiritually and emotionally. Remember being spiritually and emotionally healthy is essential for a *Sizzling Hot Marriage*.

Checking in and remaining open to the needs of your spouse along life's journey may be the single most important secret to getting and keeping the sizzle in your marriage. Who gets married to someone they plan to be unhappy with?

Nobody! Most couples start in love and are excited about their union. Or, at the very least, optimistically hopeful. Yet the reality is that the issues you both bring to the table have the potential to derail this happiness. I frequently hear couples sharing the disappointments experienced in their relationship. Certainly, you can't forget the past. Failure to do so may create an opportunity to make some of the same mistakes again. Failure to reflect on the disappointments may prevent properly processing those events. Thus, the negative impact of those disappointments may come between you and cause more problems longer than they should. But more than the disappointments, you should focus on where you are headed. Focus on what you want your marriage to be. Focus on solutions to problems rather than just the problems.

An honest look at your relationship from time to time will help you come up with great ideas that will help you make it through these bumps in the road. It will force you to look at your growth areas honestly. Couples need to learn to practice the art of being honest with one another and being open to an honest evaluation of their relationship.

Are both of you open to an honest assessment of your marriage? Are you open to your partner's negative evaluation of you?

Many people can't take criticism. I remember when I was a kid hating to hear my mother get on my case about what I hadn't done. I remember getting so heated up inside. My mind would be racing and wouldn't hear a word she said. Of course, I learned at an early age to keep some thoughts to myself. But I soon learned that a wife can be just as critical as a mother. I also learned that shutting her out is not the most effective method of handling criticism. It was difficult for me to unlearn this habit.

If you want to heat things up in your marriage, you must be mindful of where you are. You must see where you are.

Assessment includes a marital assessment and a personal assessment. The two of you need to have a frank and honest discussion about where you are in your relationship and what you are feeling personally.

It's important to periodically check in to see how things are going. Take my Hot or Not quiz [quiz.sizzlinghotmarriage. com] to see how things are going between you. Couples can quickly check in at any time to see where they are in their marriage. Taking an assessment is an important step to getting the sizzle back into your relationship.

Knowing where you are right now is imperative on any journey to any destination. One of you may be feeling like things are just fine, while the other feels that things are terrible. If you are not on the same page regarding the state of affairs, then you are not going to be on the same page as far as working on making things better.

It is easy to fall asleep in marriage, imagining that all is well. This state of denial is the preferred state for the individual who has some deep deficits that are possibly hindering the relationship. An assessment is helpful to equalize the playing field to help the couple recognize that it takes two to make a marriage what it is. I have found assessments to be very effective in helping a couple see exactly how hot their marriage is.

A SIMPLE ASSESSMENT

A simple check-in is to ask the question, "On a scale of 1 to 5, with five being the highest and one being the least, how full is your love tank?" Or "How loved do you feel?" A score of four or five is good. A one or two is bad, and three means you are on the fence. If both of you feel like you are at a four or five, you are in a good place in your marriage. If one scores high and the other is in the middle or lower, then that is significant too.

A low score suggests some dissatisfaction in the relationship that needs to be addressed. The couple must find out what needs to be done to improve things. Ask, "What are some examples of experiences with me that have led to your answer?" And then ask, "What can I do to get you up to five?" This will yield valuable information to get the sizzle back into your marriage.

Willard Harley, in his book His Needs, Her Needs, identifies ten needs that couples have in marriage. The five he identifies are primarily for women are Affection, Conversation, Honesty and Openness, Financial Support, and Family Commitment. The five he identified primarily for men include Sexual Affection, Recreational Companionship, Physical Attractiveness, Domestic Support, and Admiration.

Share with your partner where you are right now in each of these areas and what you would like that could improve your marital satisfaction. It's also important to recognize that sharing this information is not always an easy step. Many couples fail to achieve this step because the sharing of emotions is a complicated task to accomplish, as many individuals get angry when they hear what their spouse has to say. They may think that they are being unfair in their assessment, or they are not considering their contribution to the problem. This process may be so difficult that you may need a professional to help you.

You can raise your score!

If you want a *Sizzling Hot Marriage*, you must address the issues you are facing. God desires for you to be whole. Being mindful of where you are in your happy is very important to keep a *Sizzle Mindset* and keep the passion alive in your marriage.

Ryan and Tiffany now have an attitude that they will check in with each other to see how things are going. They also are committed to periodically seeking therapy to address various issues as they arise. Now that they have built a strong foundation to support their marriage, they both report much higher levels of marital satisfaction. Now that they have a *Sizzle Mindset*, they have overcome some significant hurdles, and their passion is alive and well in their marriage.

BE GOD-CENTERED

What happens when a child disobeys a wise parent's instruction? Chaos and negative consequences. Rules establish authority. Without authority, there is chaos. There are stories of matriarchal societies where the women take on the headship role in the family. However, in Western society, men have been socialized to be the head. Patriarchy has been another casualty in this current cancel-culture climate. In my opinion, the reason why patriarchy is being canceled by some is that many men have the wrong idea about what it means to lead.

First of all, leadership doesn't mean abusing those being led. Much like a waiter serves your table, leadership is an act of service. It's a role that facilitates a happy family where everyone's needs are met. Good leaders allow for role shifts as the need arises where they become the follower. Leadership does not mean all the responsibility of the relationship rests upon the leader's head. A good leader is a facilitator and guide. A bad leader is controlling and dictatorial. A good leader knows when to follow and switches roles when needed. Good leaders know who is best at what and who needs to do what in the relationship. Couples should agree on which roles they will take on in their family. Otherwise, there will be chaos.

Leadership is an essential service needed to get things done. When a leader fails to take care of the needs of his/her family, there is chaos. If there is chaos in your marriage or in your inner world, likely, you have not submitted to a set of rules that govern orderly behavior. These rules are the agreements you have made with each other. These agreements serve as the foundation for an orderly and well-managed marriage.

Too many reject the idea of an all-powerful, all-knowing, always present, and loving God. They fear judgment, control, or unobtainable expectations. Many reject the notion of God or religion because someone represented God in a harsh or abusive way. Others have difficulty comprehending the idea of a supernatural God. However, all of nature operates on the basis of rules and hierarchy. Your failure to submit to a supreme authority means you fail to recognize your limitations and responsibilities. You are out of order because authority provides us with a valuable service. When you reject God's authority, you are rejecting guidance and accountability. You will have difficulty enjoying a harmonious and mutually satisfying *Sizzling Hot Marriage* without seeking divine direction in your marriage. The closer a couple grows to God the closer they grow together. Let me encourage you to seek to understand and develop a relationship with God if you have not done so. Simply ask God to reveal Himself to you, and He will.

When considering how you measure up as a couple, you should consider what standard you are using. I believe it is essential to go back as far as possible to find the source for marital standards. Many years ago, I copied a picture I liked on a website to my website. I didn't think anything about it until one day, the picture owner contacted me and said I was infringing on their copyright of that photo. I learned then to find the original owner of a photo before posting it Online.

When we consider what our marriage should be, we must consider the originator of marriage. God himself created marriage. His ideal should be our aim and purpose.

Repeatedly studies reveal that couples with a spiritual foundation tend to enjoy more fulfilling longer lasting marriages. But to have God at the center of your marriage requires God to be the center of your life. I am confident marriages that go with God are much better able to navigate life's challenges together.

Many have a casual view of God that places very little demand on their lives. They do what they want without considering any other authority in their lives besides themselves. This is a very dangerous approach to living a life you had no part in creating. People should at least determine where they come from before deciding whether God exists or not. In my opinion, it is preferable to believe that we are intelligent beings created by an intelligent God rather than we have come from apes who resulted from a big bang in the universe. Acknowledging God's existence mandates you to live up to His rules. A solid view of God will give you a solid view of your responsibility in marriage. God will help you see marriage as more than a way to get your needs met, but rather as your marriage, and your life, fitting within the plans of God. As such, you can turn to God when you don't have the answers and trust that He is in control when you are not.

Keeping God at the center of your marriage is a remedy for success. Keeping God at the center of your marriage will keep you from making terrible mistakes that would have a devastating impact on your marriage. Keeping God at the center of your marriage will help you *Return to Love* when disappointments strike. Keeping God at the center of your marriage can keep your marital commitment solid and free from distractions.

Keeping God at the center of your marriage can only happen as both of you keep God at the center of your life. Selfishness arises as God is removed from our hearts. Marriage and selfishness are incompatible. Marriage requires selflessness. Each of you needs to assess your relationship with God.

Take a personal assessment of your relationship with God. You will have access to an unlimited source of wisdom and discernment when you allow God into your heart. Go to God for wisdom. (James 1:5) He is willing to give it to you. You should respect Him enough to ask.

There are five questions to ask yourself when assessing your spiritual health.

1. Am I moving toward God or away from God?

2. Am I living up to all I know is right to do?

3. Am I in fellowship with those who can increase my faith?

4. Am I actively pursuing God's purpose for me in service to others?

5. Can others see Jesus Christ in me?

Your spiritual connection with God plays a big part in ensuring you are doing your part to heat up your marriage. You won't be able to *Return to Love* if your heart is not in the right place. Allow God to mend your broken heart. Put everything in His hands.

In addition to a personal spiritual assessment, you should also do a personal emotional assessment. How are you doing emotionally? Your emotional health plays a major role in your marital happiness. Happy people make happy marriages. Here are five questions to ask yourself as you evaluate your emotional health.

1. Am I a happy and content individual and I feel good about myself?

2. Am I able to set and achieve goals and get my needs met healthily?

3. Am I able to enjoy reciprocal relationships inside and outside of my home?

4. Am I able to control my temper and resolve conflict peacefully?

5. Do I get adequate rest, exercise and recreation?

Your spiritual and emotional health is affected by your marital relationship. But the reverse is also true. Your marriage is affected by your spiritual and emotional health.

Ultimately, if you are going to have a *Sizzle Mindset*, you must focus on becoming a better you. If your spiritual and emotional health depends on your spouse, you are not spiritually and emotionally healthy. To get the sizzle back into your marriage, you must focus on your spiritual and emotional health. You cannot fill your spouse's love tank if you are spiritually or emotionally unhealthy. If you have some destructive behaviors, you will only drain your spouse's love tank. If your spouse has hurt you in some way, you may be holding back in some way. Being Christ-centered raises you to a high standard. It takes the focus off your spouse and on to yourself. Instead of complaining about what your spouse is or isn't doing, being Christ-centered makes you focus on making the changes you need to make. Maybe the changes you need to make will make the most significant difference in your marriage. Making yourself better is the only way your marriage will sizzle. You need to work on yourself first. God will help you if you invite Him.

REFLECTION

On a scale of 1 to 10, 10 being the highest, how consistent are you fulfilling the agreements in your marriage?

On a scale of 1 to 10, 10 being the highest, how consistent is your spouse in fulfilling their agreements in your marriage?

CHAPTER NINE
The CONCLUSION of the Matter

Don't give up on love! Make the personal changes you need to make to become better lovers. Ryan and Tiffany changed the course of their marriage because they adopted a *Sizzle Mindset*–they made love their priority and returned to loving one another even after sinning against each other. They learned the secret to a *Sizzling Hot* Marriage–Make

Love Daily! They did this by building a strong five-pillar foundation that included Credibility, Confirmation, Compassion, Community, and Consistency. They adopted the *Sizzle Mindset* to Be Hopeful, Be Committed, Be Flexible, Be Available, Be Calm, Be Talkative, Be Sexy, Be Healthy, Be Mindful, and Be God-Centered.

They kept hope alive and made it a priority to remain committed to their vow to love one another through the good times and the bad. They decided that they would not allow infidelity to distract them from their goal to face any challenge together. They determined to face every obstacle together. They remembered how God brought them together in the first place and decided to stay the course. They resolved not to allow anything to turn them away from their commitment to one another before God and witnesses on the day of their marriage.

They decided to stop trying to make the other into a carbon copy of themselves. They determined to appreciate their differences rather than make mountains out of things that would probably never change. They figured they would feel more "in love" when they both felt fully accepted. They decided to be one another's life companion instead of being each other's consummate critic. They learned how to make love and not make hate simply by being a little more flexible with each other. Both had to learn their way was not the only way. Ryan had to humble himself to listen better to his wife. What Ryan had done required Tiffany to stretch way beyond her normal limits to allow for the marriage to continue. This stretching was essential for Tiffany's personal growth and development. Both recognized their singular perspective had to change if they were to become one.

Ryan and Tiffany realized they had to put the time in if they were going to enjoy a marriage that would last their lifetime. They learned from their experience that isolation and alienation from one another wouldn't contribute to their goal of being together forever. It would only make them vulnerable for something or someone to come between them. So, they decided to spend more time together.

Ryan decided sports was not more important than his wife. He recognized that sports could never match his investment in Tiffany. Tiffany always knew how important their time together was but decided she wouldn't be so controlling about spending time together. She became more available to Ryan's ideas and timeframe.

You would never have known from the observation that Ryan and Tiffany were not experiencing a quiet and calm marriage. From the outside looking in they had it all together. While they had not engaged in violent outbursts, they had an internal storm wreaking havoc in their minds and on their relationship. Both were experiencing severe anxiety, which turned into explosive exchanges or quiet silent treatment. It was Tiffany's forgiveness of Ryan's affair that brought peace to their raging storm. This experience shook them up so that both were willing to face themselves in the mirror to figure out how this had happened. Now open to making personal changes, Ryan and Tiffany could now take their marriage to the next level. No longer burdened with anger, resentment and defensiveness, the couple could now address issues while taking responsibility for their contribution to their problems rather than just cast blame on the other. Their calmness allowed them to discuss their differences without feeling anxious inside.

Applying the mindset of being calm allowed Ryan and Tiffany to engage in open dialogue about their feelings and perspectives. Now they are much better able to talk through their disagreements without getting upset with one another. Their relationship, as with all of us, continues to develop. But they have set up some new patterns in their marriage that will be a blessing for the rest of their lives together. They now know how to communicate effectively. They know how to listen to one another. They know how to respect each other's perspectives. They know how to integrate one another's ideas into plans they both agree to follow. Being better able to talk about sensitive issues has enabled them to enjoy increased conversation with one another on many different subjects.

They can now become best friends – not just marital partners.

Since marital sex is an extension of our conversation, their improved communication has naturally led to a more enjoyable sexual experience in their marriage. Their improved communication has turned into more loving behaviors toward one another. They are more respectful of one another's love languages and, as such are feeling more loved. As the love factor has increased, so has their sexual frequency and intensity. They have many more spontaneous expressions of love because they have become more attractive to one another.

Ryan and Tiffany became healthier as they improved their ability to discuss their lifestyle and what they could do to be healthier. Ryan adjusted his sleep schedule so they could spend more time together and he would get more much-needed rest.

With these mindsets in play, Ryan and Tiffany are much more mindful of the condition of their relationship and the principles they must keep in play to stay *Sizzling Hot*. They are young and have not perfected these principles, but they have planned to keep their marriage hot by intentionally integrating these principles into their lives. They have made it their purpose to make happiness happen. They wake up thinking about their marriage. They think about each other during the day. They check in with each other daily and make sure their plans are synchronized. They are now mindful of the condition of their marriage and seek to protect their marriage through their words and actions. They are open to one another's criticism because their love tank is full. They have committed to continued therapy and assessment of their relationship. They have learned how to keep their marriage *Sizzling Hot*.

Probably most importantly, they have been intentional about keeping God at the center of their marriage. They have made time to spend time worshiping God together and having their individual devotion time. They have committed to reading the Bible together and praying together. They are making themselves prepared for the attacks of Satan by edifying their minds with the Word of God.

By understanding marriage and the difficulties that come with it, couples can work together to build a strong marriage that can withstand any challenge. It is important to remember that marriage is not something to be taken lightly and requires effort from both partners to succeed. A marriage built on mutual understanding, respect, trust, communication, commitment, and active health will result in peace, joy, and happiness for both individuals involved. With this knowledge, marriage can be an enriching and rewarding journey.

What will you do to keep the passion alive in your marriage? Will you just throw out the icebox? Will you give up on love? Or will you recognize the power you have to heat things up and bring happiness into your marriage. Make these principles a part of your mindset, and you too can have a *Sizzling Hot Marriage*. These five foundational pillars and 10 mindset shifts have the potential to turn your marriage around. Each pillar builds upon the other ensure you maintain your romance and sizzle.

The power is within you to bring happiness into your marriage. However, if both of you are willing to focus on bringing happiness into your marriage and becoming better lovers, you can have a *Sizzling Hot Marriage*?

Can the Sizzle in your marriage get hotter? Take my Hot or Not Quiz [quiz.sizzlinghotmarriage.com] to quickly assess the condition of your marriage. Don't hesitate to get professional help for your marriage. It will be time and money well spent. Why not invest in your happiness? Engaging in marriage therapy will help you work through your personal and relationship challenges exponentially faster than you would on your own. Go to GetStarted.SizzlingHotMarriage.com to complete my intake forms. I look forward to helping you restore your sizzle and build the marriage of your dreams.

If you appreciated what you have learned in my book, please take a moment to give a positive review on Amazon or wherever you purchased it. Please encourage your friends to pick up a copy as well.

READER BONUS!

Do you want a Sizzling Hot Marriage?

Get started by learning where you are right now in your relationship. I've developed a special assessment to help you identify your marriage's weak spots. This tool is a great way to see how hot or cold your marital relationship is right now. You must know where you are now to get where you want to be in your marriage. And you must periodically check in to make sure you are moving in the right direction. The wonderful thing about this quiz is that you can set it up to retake as frequently as desired. Keep moving forward toward your relationship goals.

TAKE THE QUIZ NOW!

QUIZ.SizzlingHotMarriage.com

THE SIZZLING HOT MARRIAGE MAP

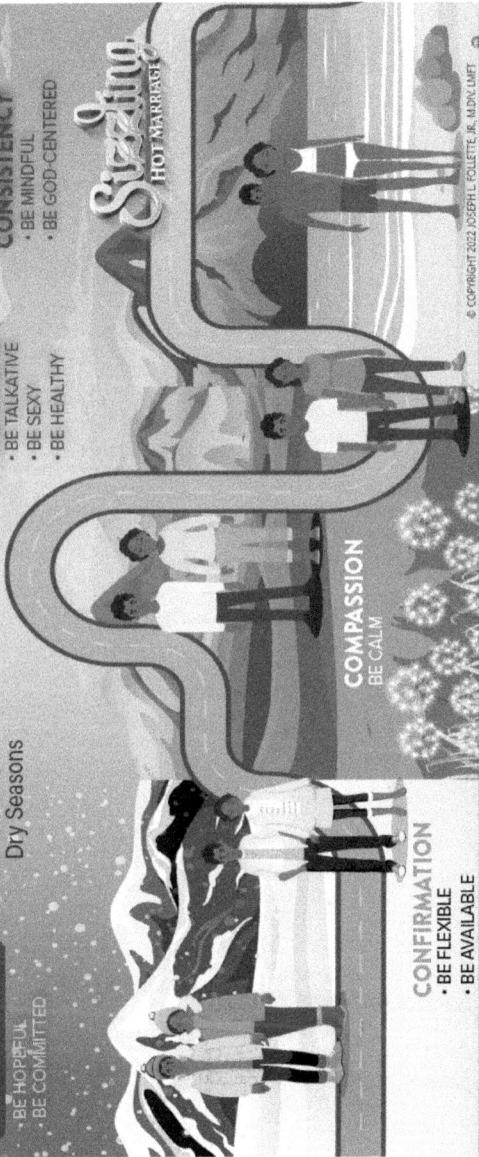

BUILD A STRONG FOUNDATION WITH THE RIGHT MINDSET FOR YOUR MARRIAGE

CREDIBILITY
- BE HOPEFUL
- BE COMMITTED

DIPS
Dry Seasons

CONFIRMATION
- BE FLEXIBLE
- BE AVAILABLE

COMPASSION
BE CALM

COMMUNITY
- BE TALKATIVE
- BE SEXY
- BE HEALTHY

CONSISTENCY
- BE MINDFUL
- BE GOD-CENTERED

Sizzling
HOT MARRIAGE

© COPYRIGHT 2022 JOSEPH L. FOLLETTE, JR., MDIV, LMFT

WARM UP YOUR MARRIAGE AT THE NEXT SIZZLING HOT MARRIAGE RETREAT
RECONNECT, RECHARGE, AND REBUILD YOUR MARRIAGE

HOW HOT IS YOUR MARRIAGE?
QUIZ.SIZZLINGHOTMARRIAGE.COM